# The Arab States and the Palestine Question

## Between Ideology and Self-Interest

# THE WASHINGTON PAPERS

. . . intended to meet the need for an authoritative, yet prompt, public appraisal of the major developments in world affairs.

**Series Editors:** Walter Laqueur; Amos A. Jordan

**Associate Editors:** William J. Taylor, Jr.; M. Jon Vondracek

**Executive Editor:** Jean C. Newsom

**Managing Editor:** Nancy B. Eddy

**Editorial Assistant:** Ann E. Ellsworth

**President, CSIS:** Amos A. Jordan

## MANUSCRIPT SUBMISSION

*The Washington Papers* and Praeger Publishers welcome inquiries concerning manuscript submissions. Please include with your inquiry a curriculum vita, synopsis, table of contents, and estimated manuscript length. Submissions to *The Washington Papers* should be sent to: *The Washington Papers*; The Center for Strategic and International Studies; Georgetown University; 1800 K Street NW; Suite 400; Washington, DC 20006. Book proposals should be sent to Praeger Publishers; 521 Fifth Avenue; New York NY 10175.

# The Arab States and the Palestine Question

## Between Ideology and Self-Interest

## Aaron David Miller

*Foreword by Alfred L. Atherton*

Published with The Center for
Strategic and International Studies,
Georgetown University, Washington, D.C.

PRAEGER SPECIAL STUDIES • PRAEGER SCIENTIFIC

New York     •     Westport, Connecticut     •     London

**Library of Congress Cataloging-in-Publication Data**

Miller, Aaron David.
  The Arab states and the Palestine question.

  (The Washington papers, ISSN 0278-937X; Vol. XIV, 120)
  "Praeger special studies. Praeger scientific."
  1. Jewish-Arab relations.  2. Palestinian Arabs —
Politics and government.  3. Near East — Politics and
government — 1945-    .  I. Georgetown University.
Center for Strategic and International Studies.  II. Ti-
tle.  III. Series.
DS119.7.M494   1986      320.956      86-931
ISBN 0-275-92215-4
ISBN 0-275-92216-2 (pbk.)

Library of Congress Catalog Card Number: 86-931
ISBN: 0-275-92215-4
ISBN: 0-275-92216-2 (pbk.)

First published in 1986

Praeger Publishers, 521 Fifth Avenue, New York, NY 10175
A division of Greenwood Press, Inc.

Printed in the United States of America

The paper used in this book complies with the Permanent
Paper Standard issued by the National Information Standards
Organization (Z39.48-1984).

10  9  8  7  6  5  4  3  2  1

# Contents

v

# Foreword

Some observers of the Middle East scene, seeking to understand the intractability of the Arab-Israeli conflict and often reflecting the perceptions of the Middle East parties themselves, frequently attribute failure to resolve that conflict to either Arab or Israeli intransigence. Others, including would-be peacemakers who have struggled with this problem over the years, have learned to view it in more complex terms, recognizing the obstacles created by political dynamics operating on both sides of the conflict and often on their own governments as well. With this has come a recognition that to depict either side of the conflict as monolithic in its views is a gross oversimplification of reality. Except for the relatively small fraternity of Middle East experts, however, recognition that this reality extends to the Palestinian Arabs has been slower in coming. Despite growing evidence in the aftermath of the 1967 Arab-Israeli war and particularly since the mid-1970s, it has only in recent years begun to be appreciated, and is still by no means generally accepted, that the Palestinians are a separate party to the conflict whose claims and views, while overlapping those of individual Arab states, are also different in many ways and are themselves not monolithic.

Aaron David Miller's earlier work, *The PLO and the*

*Politics of Survival*, reviewed the evolution, structure, and politics of the Palestinian National Movement and its institutionalization in the Palestine Liberation Organization. His present study is a timely and useful companion piece. In it Dr. Miller examines a phenomenon touched on only briefly in his previous book — the complex relationships between the Palestinians and the three Arab countries that have been the states principally party to the Arab-Israeli conflict: Jordan, Syria, and Egypt. This is a dimension of the Middle East puzzle that needs to be better understood and more fully factored into the calculations of those seeking to grapple with the intricacies of the conflict. Dr. Miller's analysis provides important insights into a question that has long baffled many observers: what are the reasons for the stubborn commitment of other Arabs to the Palestinian cause — a commitment that on the face of it would seem to have cost them dearly over the years? He examines in both historical and contemporary context the shared ideals and conflicting interests that make relations between the PLO and the governments of Jordan, Syria, and Egypt so complex, changeable, and confusing. In doing so, he illuminates a truth about the Middle East whose significance is often underestimated — namely, that the contradictions inherent in inter-Arab and particularly in Palestinian-Arab state relations are as much a part of the problem of finding a solution to the Arab-Israeli conflict as are the forces that shape the policies of the Arab and Israeli governments toward each other.

Dr. Miller's analysis in this book leads him to be skeptical about the prospects for a negotiated solution of the Israeli-Palestinian or other aspects of the Arab-Israeli conflict. That prognosis will continue to be tested in the Middle East diplomatic arena where Dr. Miller, despite his skepticism, acknowledges that progress has been made. This does not invalidate the thrust of his conclusions, which is that the constraints and imperatives confronting all the parties to the conflict, including the factors examined in this study, make the odds against further progress in the peace process very high indeed and perhaps insurmountable. Be that as it may,

Dr. Miller's dispassionate, perceptive, and clear analysis in these pages constitutes an important contribution to better public understanding of one of the most critical foreign policy issues confronting the United States today, as it has for almost four decades. If his sober prognosis proves correct, one hopes that a future study will look at what will happen in the Middle East, and in particular in Egypt and Jordan and to Egyptian-Israeli peace, in the prolonged absence of further movement toward a solution to the Arab-Israeli conflict.

Alfred L. Atherton
Former Assistant Secretary of State
for Near Eastern and South Asian Affairs

# About the Author

Aaron David Miller has been a Middle East analyst with the Department of State in the Bureau of Intelligence and Research and, in 1985, joined the secretary of state's Policy Planning Staff. During 1982–1983 he was a Council on Foreign Relations fellow and completed his most recent book, also a *Washington Paper*, on *The PLO and the Politics of Survival*. His articles have appeared in the *New York Times*, the *Los Angeles Times*, the *Washington Quarterly, Current History*, and the *Jerusalem Quarterly*. He received his Ph.D. in Middle Eastern history from the University of Michigan.

# The Arab States and the Palestine Question

## Between Ideology and Self-Interest

# 1

# Introduction

We are fed up with words and with courtesy because the
red lines are no longer known by commanders who do
not command, by kings who do not act like kings, or by
leaders who do not lead. They are no longer seen in this
empty Arab world, except in the desert, and even there
the mirage is lost.[1]
— "Voice of Palestine," Beirut, June 28, 1982

"All revolutions conceived in Palestine," the Palestine
Liberation Organization's (PLO) Salah Khalaf once remarked
to a European journalist, "have aborted in the Arab capitals."[2]
Khalaf's comment represented much more than the isolated
reflections of an embittered PLO official chased out of Jordan and at one time or another at bitter odds with Egyptian,
Syrian, and Lebanese authorities. It echoed the sentiments
of Palestinians across the political spectrum who have come
to regard the conflict of interest between the Arab states and
their own national aspirations as a basic fact of their political
life. That key Arab regimes have filled PLO coffers, facil-
itated arms purchases, and championed the Palestinian cause
in world capitals cannot obscure the bitter legacy of confrontation that has shaped their relations. It is no coincidence
that two of the PLO's most devastating defeats — King Hussein's crushing of the fedayeen in Jordan (Black September

1

1970) and Syria's battles with the Palestinians in Lebanon (Black June 1976) – have been cast by Palestinians themselves in the darkest of terms. Recent events, including Arab passivity in the face of Israel's June 1982 campaign to crush the PLO in Lebanon and the Syrian rivalry with PLO leader Yasir Arafat, suggest that the Arab world's relations with the PLO remain as controversial and stormy as ever.

Analysts and observers of varying political persuasions have been quick to focus on these tensions and to point out the sizable gap between the Arab states' rhetoric and action on the Palestinian issue. Some have tried to explain this gap by alluding to the Arabs' military weakness or their cynical manipulation of the Palestinian cause. Others see the reluctance of the Arab states to commit themselves fully in defense of the Palestinians as a calculated plot by status quo regimes to control and muzzle a revolutionary movement. The issues at stake, however, go well beyond the partisan debates waged on Arab-Israeli issues and raise important questions about one of the most complex relationships in contemporary Middle Eastern politics. What is at the heart of the Arab world's ambivalence toward the Palestinian issue? Why is there such a gap between rhetoric and action, particularly during times of crisis? What roles do ideology and self-interest play in shaping the attitudes of various Arab states? Indeed, what determines the Arab states' involvement in the Palestinian cause – a cause that has played a major role in shaping the Arab-Israeli conflict for more than half a century?

It is the central theme of this study that Egypt, Jordan, and Syria – the states most intimately involved in the Palestine problem – are bound by a common dilemma that shapes their behavior on this issue: how to reconcile their various ideological and emotional commitments and obligations to the Palestinian cause with the more sober realities of their current situation. Militarily weaker than Israel, embroiled in their own rivalries, and burdened by formidable domestic problems, these states are locked into the pursuit of Palestinian objectives they may not have the resources to achieve. Thus, the commitment to the Palestinian cause, both imposed on them by virtue of their identity and responsibilities as Arabs and voluntarily undertaken for their own narrower interests, has been impossible to discharge. In fact, an independent PLO and a Palestinian issue the Arab states cannot manage is a potential source of danger to their domestic and regional interests.

For much of the past 30 years Egypt, Jordan, and Syria have been unable to resolve this dilemma. While other Arab states, particularly Lebanon, have grappled with the consequences of an unresolved Palestinian issue, these three regimes have been the most active participants in the affairs of Palestine. All share contiguous borders with Israel, all have been active participants and lost territory in Arab-Israeli wars. And all have laid either territorial or political claims to parts of historic Palestine itself or launched major campaigns to influence the direction of the Palestinian national movement. Each state has its own perspective and stake in the Palestinian issue and has sought to pursue it in different ways. Nonetheless, there is a discernible pattern in the way these regimes have reacted.

Historically, these states have responded to the Palestinian cause on two different though inextricably connected levels. On an ideal and emotional level, the Arab states discussed in this study tend to respond collectively, rallying around time-honored and sometimes genuinely held slogans of Arab unity, independence, and support for Palestinian rights. This dimension of their involvement is generally cast as a morally uplifting crusade in which the "Arab world" as a whole is duty bound to right the injustices foisted upon Palestinians, Arabs, and Muslims by a Zionist movement backed by a colonialist West. As we shall see later, this dimension of the Palestinian issue derives its importance from the fact that it has come to embody two of the major themes — Arabism and anticolonialism — that have shaped the Arab world's political consciousness for the past half century. These themes, although interpreted by Egypt, Jordan, and Syria in the light of their historical experience, gives the Palestine issue a pan-Arab significance.

At the same time, we encounter the more concrete level.

Here Arab states have reacted not in response to an idealized conception of a pan-Arab commitment to furthering the Palestinian cause, but, individually, according to how each perceives its own interests. And here the Palestinian problem and the PLO are perceived in a more sober light: as a potential threat to these states, or as an opportunity to validate their pan-Arab credentials, outbid their rivals, and rally or distract domestic opinion. This dimension of the Arab states' involvement in the Palestinian cause is obviously far less glamorous and publicly appealing and often has to be cast in ideal terms. But it is often more consistent with the realities with which these regimes have to deal.

Nowhere are the gaps between the ideal and the real, between rhetoric and action, greater than in relations between these key Arab states and the PLO. It is probably not an exaggeration to suggest that the frontline states – Jordan, Egypt, Syria, and Lebanon – would have been far more comfortable with the Palestine issue as an abstract symbol than with the reality of an independent Palestinian movement pressing them to make good on their commitments and pursuing a strategy that has invariably created problems for these states at home and in the region. Most Arab states have accepted the fact that the PLO is the sole legitimate representative of the Palestinians and that it must somehow be co-opted or involved in a settlement. But historically, Egypt, Syria, and Jordan have worked to limit the Palestinians' independence and to tailor the PLO's goals to their own. These states remain determined to ensure that the PLO's interests remain compatible, if not subordinate, to their own interests.

Before 1967, when the military and political initiative in the Arab-Israeli conflict rested almost exclusively with the Arab states, managing this problem was less difficult. The traumatic effects of the 1967 defeat, the shattering of Palestinian and Arab confidence in the established states' abilities to confront Israel, and the emergence of a more independent Palestinian movement, however, presented a much greater challenge. Palestinian and Arab state tactics and strategies began to diverge in significant ways. The loss of territory and their own military weakness challenged Egypt and Jordan to begin considering political options to secure Israeli withdrawal.

Later, in the wake of the October 1973 war, the pan-Arab ideal of the 1950s and 1960s began to give way to a realization on the part of the frontline states and those in the Persian Gulf that the enhancement of state authority, legitimacy, and economic development was a more important challenge and a more realistic undertaking than the elusive quest for pan-Arab unity or the liberation of historic Palestine. The Arab states continued to pay tribute to the Palestinian cause, most notably at Rabat in October–November 1974 when they formally conferred on the PLO the authority it had been seeking to represent the Palestinians and to block any Jordanian or Egyptian effort to move into separate negotiations with Israel. But the October war had also convinced Egypt that to reap the benefits of its newly won military gains and to open up the door to economic development Cairo might have to be more flexible on the question of pursuing a negotiated settlement with Israel.

The gap between these two dimensions – the role various Arab states claim they would like to play in the Palestinian arena and the role they more frequently act out – carries important implications for the Arab-Israeli conflict and for their own domestic and regional policies. First, because identification with the Palestinian cause plays such an important normative role in enhancing a regime's legitimacy, Arab states have traditionally wrapped themselves tightly in the Palestinian flag. Although this association is often useful in boosting a regime's prestige at home and its influence in the Arab world, it severely limits the flexibility of those states interested in moving into a negotiated settlement with Israel. Should negotiations actually begin, most likely between Jordan and Israel, Jordanian maneuvering room would be reduced by Palestinian desiderata and by pressure from rival regimes seeking to use Palestinian demands to undercut King Hussein's position.

The second consequence flows from the first. Even though

key Arab states have sought strength and protection in associating with the Palestinian cause, the dichotomy between what these regimes are prepared to say in defense of the Palestinians and what they are prepared to do is an acute source of vulnerability and embarrassment. No other issue forces them to recognize their own limitations and weaknesses more. And no other issue provides more effective ammunition for their domestic opponents and regional rivals. The fear of betraying Palestinian interests by negotiating with Israel makes it difficult for any regime to depart from the Arab consensus on such a core issue. Egyptian President Anwar Sadat's willingness to go it alone, resulted from unique circumstances that will be difficult for other Arab states to follow.

Third, the gap between an Arab state's rhetoric and action has afforded the PLO a surprising amount of leverage and further reduced a regime's room to maneuver. Although the Palestinians are dangerously dependent on their Arab patrons, PLO support is viewed as an essential asset in competing in the inter-Arab arena or, as the Jordanians have discovered, in laying the groundwork for negotiations with Israel. Recognizing its leverage, the PLO has sought to ensure that Arab regimes do not deviate from the established Arab consensus or betray Palestinian goals. Moreover, adherence to the maximalist interpretation of that consensus serves the interests of radical Palestinian groups and plays into the hands of those regimes that see no urgency or need for a negotiated settlement with Israel.

Fourth, the gap between rhetoric and action only reinforces the tension between conservative Arab states fearful of radical changes in the status quo and a Palestinian movement determined to alter it. Although the PLO has moderated its own goals over the past decade, it is still committed to a revolutionary change in the current situation – the establishment of another Arab state in a highly volatile area. Although none of the states discussed in this study are opposed in principle to the fulfillment of Palestinian national goals, all are determined to ensure that in the process of fulfillment, Palestinian interests are compatible with, if not subordinate to, their own concerns. The fact that these states frequently have to maintain the illusion that they are supporting an independent state and the PLO — while doing everything they can to prevent too independent a PLO from jeopardizing their own interests — only heightens the tensions between them.

Short of a comprehensive solution to the Arab-Israeli conflict based on favorable terms for all parties, reconciling the ideal and real dimensions of the Palestinian problem may not be possible. If, in a vacuum sheltered from internal pressures and inter-Arab rivalries, each of these regimes could settle equitably with Israel, such a reconciliation might be possible. But the Palestinian issue seems too inextricably linked to the long-term stability of Jordan and Lebanon and so interwined with Syria's image and interests in the region that finding a solution compatible with these diverse pressures and interests, which is also acceptable to Israel, will be extremely difficult. Without a significant softening in the positions of Israel, key Arab states, and the Palestinians themselves, the "Arab commitment" to the Palestinian cause will probably continue at a strong enough level to prevent negotiated settlements, but not at a powerful enough level to force a settlement on terms favorable to these states or to the Palestinians. Egypt has gone further than any other Arab state in successfully reconciling this dilemma. Yet even here an unresolved Palestinian problem will continue to threaten Cairo's gains. For Syria, an unresolved Palestinian issue is probably manageable, some might even argue desirable. But for Jordan, it poses a fundamental threat to the stability and security of the Hashemite regime. And it is Egyptian and Jordanian interests that will suffer most from an indefinite continuation of the status quo. Indeed, these two states — and perhaps in the end Syria as well — may remain burdened by a cause that leaves them far short of accomplishing their political or territorial objectives, trapped somewhere between seeing their world as it is and how they would like it to be.

# 2

## The Palestine Issue as Ideology

The Palestinian Revolution is an Arab Dream[3]
— Salah Khalaf

The Palestinian cause in which the Arab states have now been involved for more than half a century is based on their view that Western-backed European Zionists usurped Arab territory, displaced its inhabitants, and established a Jewish state in the heart of Arabdom. Few ideas seem to have attracted as diverse a constituency or affected the internal politics and foreign policies of most Arab states in more profound ways. Although, as we shall see, this commitment has been given remarkably flexible interpretations and has been adjusted to coincide with the interests of various Arab states, it has become a permanent feature of the area's ideological landscape. Embued with political and religious symbolism, the Palestine issue has left a deep mark on what remains of the collective Arab consciousness — acting as a major catalyst in the rise of Arab nationalism and reflecting the Arab states' sensitivities on a variety of issues from anticolonialism to the lack of political legitimacy confronting most of these regimes.

What makes the Arab states' relationship with the Palestinian cause so complex is that although the commitment to the cause has been compromised by Arab actions over the years, it remains for many a relatively untarnished political ideal. Whatever their motives, Arab politicians, intellectuals, and religious thinkers from Morocco to Iraq have helped to elevate the Palestinian issue to an almost sacred level in their political culture. The issue dominates Arab summits, has free reign at the United Nations, and fills the revolutionary communiqués of Iraqi Ba'thists and the mosque sermons of conservative Saudi ulama alike. No Arab leader can afford to ignore its popular appeal and the special obligations and problems that it poses. Indeed, there seems to be a pervasive feeling in the area that those who compromise Palestinian goals, let alone move toward accommodation with Israel, will meet the same fate as Jordan's King Abdullah, Lebanon's Bashir Gemayel, and Egypt's Anwar Sadat.

To a great extent the salience of the Palestinian issue has resulted from the Arab world's refusal to come to grips with the broader question of the existence of the state of Israel. Most Arab regimes perceived the creation of a Jewish state and the displacement of the Palestinian Arabs as two sides of the same coin. For almost three decades this perception—that as long as there was an Israel there would be a Palestinian problem—has persisted. Although for most Arab states the nature of the debate has now shifted from a discussion of Israel's existence to the issue of its boundaries, resolution of the Palestinian issue remains the sine qua non for formal recognition of Israel. Even Egypt, which has concluded a formal treaty of peace with Israel, seems to have made the full development of relations contingent on progress on this issue.

The resilience of the Palestinian problem received another giant boost from the Arab regimes' search for political legitimacy and the insecurities and weaknesses that flowed from a precarious domestic base. As some have noted, Arab politicians from Saudi Arabia to Syria have operated in a political environment where the legitimacy of rulers, regimes, and institutions were at best scarce.[4] In this atmosphere, highly charged with revolutionary, religious, and nationalist values, Arabs could not afford to be outflanked on issues and causes that carried great popular appeal. In the hands of opposition elements and rival regimes, issues such as the Palestine cause presented powerful weapons that could be used to enhance or to discredit the legitimacy and authority of the state. Riding the tiger of Palestinian nationalism was a risky but necessary business for these regimes and inevitably reinforced an extremism and maximalism that would become part of their basic approach to the Arab-Israeli conflict.

Playing the Palestine issue as good politics goes a considerable distance toward explaining its resilience in the Arab world. But it does not go far enough. The commitment to the Palestinian cause was more than just an artificially contrived political weapon to be used at home and in the inter-Arab arena by insecure and weak regimes. Indeed, it was precisely because this issue struck such strong chords and touched on popularly perceived grievances that it had to be managed and controlled by regimes that were not at all confident about their political base. The more these regimes managed this issue in an attempt to keep the Palestinian issue ablaze, but at a degree at which they themselves would not get burned, the more entrenched and established the idea of their commitment to the cause became: Whether or not these regimes were judged by Palestinians or their own publics to be either inept or less than committed to the Palestinian quest was not the issue. What mattered was that these regimes were expected to remain engaged on this issue and to try to measure up to the standards they themselves had set.

Since the early 1970s, the tempering of maximal Arab goals and the sobering of attitudes has to some degree broken this vicious cycle. Realization on the part of most contemporary Arab leaders that Israel cannot be destroyed by military force, the need to concentrate on enhancing their own political authority and economic development, and the shock of Egypt's decision to withdraw from the confrontation line with Israel have had a sobering impact on most regimes' view of their role in the conflict and particularly on what is possible on the Palestinian issue. But these factors have by no means eroded the Palestinian issue's power to prevent negotiated settlements with Israel. What to do about the Palestinians still occupies a prominent feature in the Arab states' planning and calculations on the resolution of the Arab-Israeli conflict.

What is it then that gives the Palestinian issue such enduring value and resiliency in Arab political culture? That various regimes have tried to manipulate the issue has not diminished its impact or effect in the streets and among the public at large. The Palestinian issue remains a vibrant force because it encapsulates two basic themes that have shaped the Arab world's political experience for half a century: a shared identity as Arabs and independence from foreign influence. These elements are not just abstract, superficial ideas manipulated by politicians and bandied about by intellectuals; they strike deep and responsive chords throughout the Arab world. In fact, they embody the aspirations of millions of Arabs who, despite their differences, still take pride and satisfaction in sharing a common language, a cultural tradition, and the elements of a common historical experience. As we shall see, various Arab states have accorded these elements a different weight and value depending on their particular interests and orientation. But to a great extent they have transcended political and geographic boundaries. Moreover, they have roots that extend deep into the Arab past. Indeed, it is precisely this continuity that gives these themes, and thus the Palestinian cause, a unique source of durability and strength. And it is to these general themes that we now turn.

## Alone Together: Arab Unity and the Palestinian Cause

As recently as 1978, a highly respected Palestinian scholar noted that the Arab states' system is a "pan" system, postulating the existence of a single Arab nation behind the facade of a multiplicity of sovereign states.[5] That contemporary Middle Eastern politics in the last 50 years has revealed an Arab world acting precisely in the opposite fashion, each nation attending to its own interests at the expense of the Arab nations and the Palestinian cause, does not obscure the popular attraction of such an ideal. The tendency to interpret reality in ways that are consonant with an appealing self-image exists in all societies. And in the Arab world the proposition that the Arabs should be a united nation was strengthened by powerful cultural, religious, and geographic factors that seemed to pull it together. A common language — Arabic — and a common religion — Islam — acted as powerful mechanisms for identification and the transmission of a cultural and intellectual heritage that carried the potential to shape a common outlook. Moreover, geography also appeared to favor the idea of a unified whole, providing a network of contiguous Arab-speaking lands from North Africa to the Arabian Peninsula and northeast across the Levant.

As if this were not enough to power the dream, the entire region, while divided into subregions each with its own particular characteristics, grappled with many of the same general problems of foreign domination and, more recently, the challenges of modernization and development. For centuries in the Arab Levant — comprising today's states of Jordan, Syria, Iraq, and Lebanon — the lack of organic identities as independent states increased the area's susceptibility to ideas that offered a strong sense of identity, purpose, and attachment. With no strong affiliation to local nationalisms, it was almost inevitable that a broader movement offering a special sense of mission and destiny would find adherents. Commenting on the unique source of power available to the Arabs, Gamal Abdel Nasser, who would later harness the power of pan-Arabism to establish himself and Egypt as preeminent forces in the region, noted in his *Philosophy of the Revolution*, "we are a group of neighboring peoples joined together with such spiritual and material bonds as can join any group of peoples."[6] It would have been unthinkable that such a unique and appealing call would have gone unanswered. Charismatic leadership and the call of destiny offered an unbeatable combination certain to attract millions and to fill any ideological or spiritual void.

Almost from the beginning the commitment to the Palestinian cause reflected this pan-Arab ideal while making effective cooperation on the issue difficult to achieve. The inability of the Arabs of Palestine to organize effectively, the dependence on their neighbors' diplomatic influence, and, indeed, the lack of a clearly defined sense of Palestinian national identity contributed to the common perception that what was happening in Palestine from 1917 to 1948 was an Arab problem. Increasing Jewish immigration, British support for the idea of a Jewish homeland embodied in the Balfour Declaration, and the establishment of viable Zionist economic and political institutions represented in the minds of many not only a threat to the Arabs of Palestine but also to Arabs everywhere. As early as the 1930s, Egyptian commentators were already warning that Jewish dominance would threaten the "unity of the Arab East" or, worse, would constitute the "greatest barrier to the Arabs joining of their capabilities, the uniting of their efforts, and their cooperation."[7]

While Arab regimes were already working to exploit the pan-Arab dimension of the Palestinian cause and use it for their own purposes, the idea of the *qadiyat* (the "issue") as an all-Arab concern was gaining momentum.[8] Nasser recounts that the first elements of his "Arab consciousness" began to filter into his mind as a student during the annual demonstrations protesting the issuance of the Balfour Declaration. During the interwar period, the Arab states, in an effort to impose some semblance of order on a divided Palestinian movement and to influence Great Britain, became increasingly active in diplomatic efforts on behalf of Palestinian Arabs. And the 1936–1939 Arab rebellion evoked widespread sympathy throughout the region. Following the UN vote in favor of the 1947 partition plan, a wave of demonstrations and violence swept through the Arab world. In Baghdad, Aleppo, and Aden, Jews were killed, and homes, shops, and synagogues destroyed.[9]

But it was the events of 1948 and 1949 that dramatically intensified the pan-Arab dimension of the Palestinian issue. Before 1948 the Arab states' stake and involvement in the

Palestine question was diffuse and hard to define. The establishment of a Jewish state, the divisions within Arab ranks, and the pitiful performance of the Arab armies linked the confrontation states in a common bond of humiliation and defeat. Events in Palestine went well beyond the defeat of Palestinian Arabs and were interpreted as an Arab debacle on every level. The Arab regimes and armies had boasted of their plans to crush a Jewish state and had staked their prestige at home on the success of this campaign. Thus, the debacle in Palestine undermined the confidence and credibility of these regimes and helped to destroy what little legitimacy they had achieved among their own constituents.

As Fayez Sayegh, a Palestinian writer and activist noted,

> to millions of Arabs the loss of Palestine was the indictment of a whole generation. The import of that harsh verdict went beyond Palestine, beyond military power or impotence: it was a judgement on values cherished for thirty years, on premises of thought axiomatic since the end of the First World War, on age-old traditions and systems of social organization, in short, on an entire mode of existence.[10]

Thus, events in Palestine served as a catalyst to intensify the debate on the need for fundamental changes at home and in foreign policy. Within four years, most of the leaders of the 1948–1949 Arab war coalition had been either assassinated or ousted from power.

However traumatic and divisive the impact of the *al-naqba* (the disaster) was for the credibility and unity of the Arab states, it strengthened their resolve and determination in other ways. The debacle in Palestine created a new set of powerful myths and images centered around the need to erase the shame and dishonor created by the defeat. The loss of Palestine, viewed as an integral part of the Arab world and the link between the Arab east and west, was invariably elevated to a defeat for the entire Arab world. The defeat generated a new set of ideals and objectives intended to explain and rationalize the Palestine episode and resulted in a new set of challenges focused on the importance of a unified Arab response in the future. After 1948 it seemed unthinkable that the Arab states — who perceived themselves as the aggrieved parties — could conceive of any compromise with Israel except from a position of strength. Nor would there be any defections from the ranks. As Fouad Ajami notes, having vowed to undo the shame of the defeat, it became difficult for any state to take itself out of the conflict.[11]

Although the Palestinian defeat generated a large amount of realistic self-criticism by intellectuals and politicians, it tended to reinforce rather than diminish the importance of Palestine as a pan-Arab cause. One of the major themes reflected in the cathartic outpouring over Palestine was the view that Arab disunity had played a key role in the defeat. This disunity was attributed to numerous factors, including inept and corrupt Arab leadership and Western plots. Instead of producing a more realistic and pragmatic view of the inherent contradictions and problems of working toward a unified Arab position, it produced precisely the opposite reaction. If only the Arab states could unify and overcome the political and historical differences that divided them, it was argued, they could succeed against Zionism and the West. It was no coincidence that Nasser, who formulated and exploited the pan-Arab ideal to assert his own influence and move Egypt to center stage, emphasized the importance of learning from the Palestine episode. "The tragedy of Palestine was a victory for the Arabs," Nasser declared in 1959, "for it lit the fire of Arab nationalism . . . and aroused the Arab conscience in every country."[12] Palestine was not the only catalyst in the search for Arab unity during the 1950s and 1960s, but it provided much of the rationalization for the abortive unity schemes of the period.

The importance of Arab unity in the commitment to the Palestinian cause was a particularly effective theme for politicians to exploit because it was grounded in the public perception of how Arab regimes should behave and in the expectations and goals they set for themselves. In this sense the commitment to the Palestinian cause provided a role for the Arabs to play that was consonant with their own self-image. Regardless of their differences, the Arab states had a vision of history and of the future based on a sense of devotion, sacrifice, honor, and, for many, a religiously determined destiny. The Palestine issue was, as Algerian President Houari Boumediene stated, the "symbol of the honor of the Arab nation."[13] Or in the words of King Hussein, "the Palestine question is the cause of the Arab nation. It is the Arab right."[14] Given the importance of this concept and its relationship to Arab self-esteem and dignity, the honor had to be redeemed. In fact, in the wake of the 1967 defeat, the Palestinian fedayeen themselves became symbols of the importance of saving the collective Arab face. With Nasser's image tarnished, the fedayeen emerged as the "new men" committed to principle, and, as their name suggested, they sought to "sacrifice themselves" in the pursuit of reclaiming Palestinian rights and Arab honor. It made little difference that the Palestinian fedayeen were soon tarnished by the same faults and overblown rhetoric of their Arab patrons; the act of resistance itself provided an attractive and appealing psychological boost for a demoralized Arab world.[15]

It was really not important that the beliefs and ideas underpinning this self-image be consistent with present day realities. Arab politicians frequently reached deep into the past for many of the associations and images in which they wrapped their involvement in the Palestinian cause. References to Salah al-Din, the Crusaders, and the triumph of Arab nationalism over colonial rule filled the national day speeches and communiqués of Palestinian and Arab leaders. That the Arab regimes continued to lose prestige and territory in their political and military bouts with Israel was not as important as the perception that the struggle was continuing. Although the Arab states might be beaten again and again, as the 1948, 1956, and 1967 conflicts revealed, there was a clear feeling that they would never surrender. If these regimes could not wage a successful war against Israel, then at least they could deny the Jewish state the benefits of a real peace.

## The Palestine Issue, Colonialism, and
## the Search for Arab Independence

If the commitment to the Palestinian cause reflected an infatuation, if not a full blown love affair, with pan-Arabism, it also represented the Arab states' hypersensitivity to foreign influence and the desire to assert their independence from outside forces. This was not a new problem. For centuries before the creation of the modern Arab states and the establishment of Israel, the Arab world had grappled with the challenges of dealing with a variety of hostile forces — Eastern and Western — that had intruded into their world. As they looked back on their history, Arab intellectuals must have interpreted the experience as an extremely painful one. After the collapse of the Arab empire, which at its peak had stretched from the Atlantic and the Pyrenees in the west to the borders of India and China in the east, the Arabs were generally on the defensive, confronting an array of hostile forces from a position of military and political weakness. Even the Ottomans, whose administrative, political, and military skills sustained an empire for almost seven centuries, failed to resolve the problems posed by the challenges of a technologically superior and expansive West. When the Ottoman Empire collapsed in the aftermath of World War I, the challenge of how to deal with Britain, France, and Russia again became the responsibility of Arab provinces that were uncertain of their own identities and burdened by centuries of exploitation and neglect.

The experience of the Arab provinces and national movements under the French and British mandates need not detain us here. Suffice it to say that, given European political and strategic interests and Britain's involvement with political Zionism, conflict with Arab national movements struggling to achieve greater control over their own affairs and wrestling with enormous social and economic problems at home was inevitable. Whether the various Arab nationalist movements were betrayed by British promises of support, blinded by their own passions, or misled by ambiguous commitments to Arab independence misses the point. What the Arab world inherited from the Ottomans was a problem that had remained unresolved for centuries. It was more than just a modern day "Eastern Question" concerned with filling the vacuum created by a collapsing empire. The issues at stake represented nothing short of a fundamental clash between opposing cultures and civilizations. The West — Christian, expansive, and in a stage of dynamic growth and development — confronted a traditional, Islamic Arab world struggling with tremendous social, economic, and political problems with which its leaders were not equipped to deal. Not only had the Arabs been unable to relate to a variety of outside forces on equal terms, but they also had been despised and dominated by outside forces for centuries. The contempt the West often exhibited toward the Arabs, Albert Hourani wrote, "was all the more unbearable to the Arabs because of their conviction that in essentials they were not inferior to the west, no less than their suspicion that in many other things they were indeed far behind the west and had much to learn from it."[16]

Each of the countries discussed in this study had different experiences with the Western powers with which they came into contact and sought to resolve the conflicts between them in different ways. Nonetheless, their struggle for independence shaped their political experiences between the two world wars and continued to influence their attitudes and actions long after formal independence. The anticolonialist sentiment fed the wave of pan-Arabism that swept the Middle East during the 1950s and 1960s. Arab nationalists of every stripe rallied around the theme of Western penetration and exploitation and hammered home the connection between Israel and Western support.

During these years, however, the Arab states' relationship with the West was beginning to change in important ways. The decline of European influence in the Middle East was already evident following the end of World War II and plummeted dramatically after the Suez crisis in 1956. Nor had the United States yet achieved the level of influence and involvement in the area that it would enjoy by the early

1970s. During these years, Arab regimes became more assertive and confident and began to relate to their former over-
lords on a more equal basis. Following the 1973 war and the
oil embargo, some Arab states began to believe that they now
had more leverage over the Europeans and even the United
States. Although the fear of Western penetration and anti-
imperialist rhetoric remained strong, most Arab regimes
began to tailor their ideological passions to their own self-
interest. This process had been in train for at least half a century and had characterized relations between the European
powers and traditional elites in Iraq, Egypt, Jordan, and
Saudi Arabia. What was noteworthy about the changing attitude toward the West was that this wave now included regimes
who prided themselves on the purity of their Ba'thist and
revolutionary Arab nationalist credentials. These regimes
jealously guarded their independence, but they seemed much
more pragmatic and mature in their dealings with the Western powers, even with the United States.

The process of decolonization in the Middle East and the
Arab states' relations with the Western powers might have
been no more complicated than similar processes elsewhere
had it not been for the strange case of Palestine. It cannot
be emphasized strongly enough that the Palestine problem
was not the sole basis of the tensions between the Arab states
and the West. As I have noted before, relations foundered
on a fundamental clash of religious and political values and
contrasting perceptions of motives and interests. Nonetheless, in the Arab view, the Palestine problem strengthened
and exacerbated preexisting tensions and guaranteed that
they would outlast the last vestiges of the colonial experience.
The creation of a Jewish state in the heart of the Arab world
and the Arabs' inability to do anything about it quickly became a symbol of the East's impotence and the West's disregard for Arab sensitivities and aspirations.

Despite the ambivalence that characterized the Arabs'
view of Europe and the United States and the willingness of
key Arab states to enter into close relations with the United
States, Israel's primary supporter, the Palestine cause be-

came synonymous with Western exploitation and influence. Without Western support, many Arabs rationalized, Israel could not have been created or survived in so hostile a climate. Worse still, the Palestine issue came to represent Arab weakness and reflected a lack of unity and resolve. The state of Israel became a kind of mirror in which the Arab regimes daily saw a reflection of their own powerlessness and the superiority of Western ways. Israel constantly reminded the Arabs that whatever their past glories and accomplishments, they were now impotent and weak.

From the perspective of the Arab nationalists, unsure of their own identities, struggling with an array of formidable economic and social problems, and burdened with a legacy of foreign penetration, it was easy to see how the Palestine question could become identified with hostility toward the West, particularly toward the United States. First, the Palestine problem gave Arab hostility a much more focused character. While each Arab regime had waged its own battle with a particular mandatory power — Syria and Lebanon with the French, Egypt and Iraq with the British — the Palestine problem provided a common target for venting the Arabs' nationalist and pan-Arab spleen, first against Britain, author of the Balfour Declaration, and, then, as the European powers became more sympathetic to Palestinian and Arab interests, against the United States as primary benefactor of Israel. The fact that some of these regimes also had a stake in maintaining close ties with the United States was all the more frustrating and potentially dangerous. The Palestine issue provided a powerful weapon for radical opposition elements, the Palestinians themselves, and rival regimes to attack states such as Jordan, Egypt, and Saudi Arabia for dealing with the enemies of the Palestinian people. Indeed, the lowest common denominator style of politics that still characterizes Arab politics made the Palestine cause a perfect issue for this kind of manipulation.

Second, although Arab regimes clearly used the Palestine issue to divert the attention of Arab publics from the regimes' failures to cope with the enormous political, economic, and social problems at home, the connection of Palestine with imperialism was already a popular idea in the minds of alienated and embittered intellectuals, political activists, and common folk who saw the world in essentially conspiratorial terms. For many, Israel provided a base and foothold for the extension of U.S. influence and control throughout the Middle East.

However outrageous an assumption, the view that Israel and imperialism were linked in a kind of unholy alliance shaped Arab perceptions for years. "Israel is an aggressive base in the service of imperialism," the Egyptian commentator Muhammed Hassanein Heykal wrote in 1964, "so that it could serve as a point of departure from which it could leap whenever it wanted to strike and oppress. . . . "[17] Or in the words of the Arab propagandist M. T. Mehdi,

> Of course the problem was that the Arabs were not fighting little Israel alone. They were fighting the combined might of western Europe and North America and all the support given to the Jewish state by the western world. The Arabs were fighting *Thanab Al-Hayyah*, the tail of the snake, in Palestine, while its head — *Raas Al-Hayyah* — was in the United States of America.[18]

Twenty years later the rhetoric and many of the basic assumptions remained strikingly similar. "We in the Arab region," Syrian President Hafiz al-Assad noted in late 1983, "are facing a Zionist imperialist design that is aimed at dominating the region."[19]

Third, for the Arabs, the Palestine problem went beyond the traditional colonial experience and represented more than an imposition of an alien regime and administration.[20] However permanent the League of Nations' mandates may have appeared at the time, it was always assumed that British and French control would be temporary. Even in the case of the British occupation of Egypt, Egyptian nationalists always believed that the negative effects of British influence could be ameliorated once the British departed.

Not so with the Palestine issue. To the Arabs, the emergence of political Zionism initially represented a threat to the fabric of Arab social, economic, political, and religious life. The creation of Israel not only resulted in the displacement of hundreds of thousands of Palestinian Arabs but the establishment of an alien state in their midst. Throughout the 1950s, Arab polemicists and intellectuals spoke of Israel as a wedge in the center of the Arab world that would disrupt its development and frustrate any hope of unity. Although some have tried to rationalize the problem away by comparing Israel to the Crusaders or to a number of other foreign intruders who had eventually passed from the scene, the stronger the Israelis became and the more permanent their institutions, the more resigned these states became to the fact that Israel was not about to disappear any time soon. Many Arabs and Palestinian ideologues who push the view that time is on their side have still not accepted this fact, however. But whatever their ideal hopes, the states discussed in this study — Egypt, Jordan, and Syria — now base their policies on the assumption that Israel is here to stay. That these regimes have accepted this fact, however, does not mean they are willing to abandon their territorial and political objectives. Indeed, the Arab states believe that they have already made enormous concessions in accepting the existence of Israel within the pre-1967 borders and believe that the major responsibility for further steps in any negotiated solution must come from Israel.

Finally, what made the situation worse and exacerbated feelings of shame and humiliation with regard to Palestine was that the Arab states were being beaten by Jews. It was one thing to be locked in combat and dominated by the West's greatest powers. There was even a certain virtue in the competition even if one lost. But to be beaten by those who historically have been regarded at best as a second class minority or, worse, with a mixture of hostility and contempt was clearly another matter. For many Arabs, the terms Jews and Israelis are still used interchangeably, and anti-Semitic stereotypes are still evident in the Arab press.

Moreover, the fact that the Israelis had succeeded in cap-
turing East Jerusalem and restoring the city to what they
believed to be its preeminent place in the Jewish history,
culture, and religion only heightened the political and religious tensions between Arabs and Israelis. It is impossible to underestimate both the Arab and Muslim feeling on
this issue and the importance the Arab states attach to regaining control over at least East Jerusalem. Various states
accord the Jerusalem issue a different value according to
their particular orientation. For the Saudis, as protectors of
Mecca and Medina, the fate of Islam's third holiest city is
particularly important. And for Jordan's King Hussein, whose
country's entry into the 1967 war shackled the Hashemites
with the loss of yet another holy city, Jerusalem is also a core
issue. Indeed, for the Arabs as a whole – Muslim and Christian alike – the Jerusalem issue will remain a crucial ingre-
dient in any resolution of the Arab-Israeli conflict. Indeed,
it is no coincidence that the Arab states' initial diplomatic
involvement in the Palestine question was sparked by the
1929 wailing wall riots and their concern over the fate of the
Muslim holy places.

The concepts of Arabism and Arab independence have
shaped the Arab world's view of itself, each other, and the
outside world in important ways. To a certain extent, these
ideas, as they are reflected in the Palestinian issue, have
transcended political, sectarian, and geographic divisions and
have provided elements of a common approach to the Palestinian problem. Nonetheless, it would be misleading to suggest that this ideological dimension of the Palestinian issue
affected the Arab states in the same way. Different historical
experiences and political and demographic factors gave Jordan, Syria, and Egypt their own perspective on the problem
of Palestine and shaped their individual approaches to the
issue. Each of these countries interpreted their Arabism and
their relationship to foreign powers in their own way. Indeed,
any ideology is essentially a specific interpretation of reality.
And these states were bound to interpret their experiences
in different ways. It is to this subject that I now turn.

# 3

# Jordan and the Palestinian Cause: A Family Affair

> For us the Palestinian question is a question of life or death, a cause of right, a cause of message, an Arab cause which we had the honor to defend.[21]
>
> — King Hussein

Nowhere is the line between ideology and self-interest more tenuous than in the history of Jordan's involvement in the affairs of Palestine. Jordan's critical stake in resolving the Palestinian problem in a way that is compatible with its own security and sovereignty frequently obscures the more abstract and subjective factors that have shaped the Hashemites' involvement in this issue for more than half a century. Middle East analysts consistently point out the demographic, political, and geographic imperatives that link Jordan's fate to the Palestinian issue and almost always present the relationship in negative terms—either as a threat or a burden that the regime cannot ignore. The Hashemites are portrayed as trapped between the forces of an unrequited and radical Palestinian nationalism and the demographic pressures of a Palestinian majority on the East Bank. Throughout all of this hangs the ominous specter of another Arab-Israeli war that could undermine the monarchy.

Jordan's concerns and fears are valid enough. Despite the

24

arguments of those who believe that Hashemite interests might be better served by forgetting about the Palestinian cause and concentrating on the East Bank, it is clear that the Jordanians cannot run from a problem that concerns both banks of the Jordan River. This realization has provided great continuity in the policies of Abdullah and Hussein and has challenged the Hashemite kings to assuage, exploit, and contain Palestinian national aspirations. Nonetheless, what is often overlooked in this realpolitik interpretation is the role that less rational factors, such as ideology and prestige, have played in shaping the Hashemite kings' view of their Palestinian dilemma. Why did Abdullah feel so strongly about the area west of the Jordan River in the first place? And why has his grandson been so committed to regaining the territory that caused his grandfather so much trouble and, some would say, cost Abdullah his life? The answers to these questions are paradoxically linked to the same demographic, political, and geographic factors that have made the case for Jordanian involvement in the Palestinian cause so compelling. But they also lend themselves to a more subjective interpretation of the Hashemites' interest in Palestine—an interest that is related to their own authority and prestige in the Arab world, their self-image, and, in Hussein's case, the loss of the West Bank and East Jerusalem in 1967. Although these factors are not easy to measure, they have given the Palestine issue a unique hold and attraction for both Jordanian monarchs and provided Hussein in particular with a great personal stake in seeing it resolved.

Few would disagree that the Hashemite Kingdom of Jordan has a connection to the Palestine problem unmatched by any other Arab state. Even Syria, which claims that Palestine was carved from its own territory, cannot rival the bonds that tie the Hashemites to the area west of the Jordan River. These bonds are not only historical but are intimately linked to Jordan's present and future. Between 1948 and 1967 Jordan alone controlled a vital part of historic Palestine and, unlike Egypt's control of Gaza, incorporated the West Bank into its own territory. Moreover, the links were not only to the territory but to the tenants. Abdullah and Hussein established unique relationships with Palestinians there and on the East Bank. And of all the Arab states, only Jordan granted citizenship en masse to the refugees and inhabitants that resided within its borders after 1948 and 1967. Despite the limitations and restrictions imposed on Palestinians, they were integrated into East Bank life in a way unparalleled elsewhere. More than 1 million Palestinians (one-quarter of the world's total) now reside in Jordan — a fact that by itself makes the Palestinian issue more salient for Jordan than for any other Arab state.

It should not be surprising that so vital a connection was bound up with the origins and development of the Emirate of Transjordan, predecessor of the current Jordanian state. Until World War I, the area east of the Jordan River lacked a defined territorial or national identity. With the destruction of the Ottoman Empire, most of the territories formerly governed from Istanbul were caught up in French-British maneuvering for control of the Levant. According to a series of wartime agreements between Paris and London, sanctioned unwittingly by a League of Nations system of mandates, Britain received stewardship of Palestine and Iraq and France of Syria and Lebanon. The settled area east of the Jordan River, most of which had been occupied by British forces in 1918, was given three years later provisionally to Abdullah, son of Sharif Hussein of Mecca, nominal leader of the British-backed Arab revolt.

The arrangements, formalized at the Cairo conference of 1921, were intended to pacify Abdullah, who appeared determined to move into Syria to support his younger brother Faisal, whom the French had recently thrown out of Damascus. These were problems the British Colonial Office did not need. Moreover, it was also evident to Winston Churchill, then head of the Colonial Office, that this area was too important strategically as a land bridge to Iraq and the Persian Gulf, too cumbersome an area to be included profitably in the mandate for Palestine, and too potentially useful a tool in manipulating the Arab nationalists to be ignored. Having considered the displaced Faisal for the Iraqi throne, the British thought to install his brother in Amman. Besides, what better way to soothe Arab anger over the Balfour Declaration, keep the Zionists in their place, and hedge their bets against the French than to set up another Arab client with ties to Britain.[22] In a 1946 treaty, Great Britain recognized Transjordan as an independent state with Abdullah as its ruler.

Despite the formal separation of Transjordan from the Palestine mandate in 1922, a fact Abdullah intellectually acknowledged, he never really relinquished his dream of uniting both banks of the Jordan both as an end in itself and as a stepping stone to his ultimate goal of a Greater Syria based in Damascus comprising Palestine and Transjordan. Palestine presented a natural direction for the promotion of Hashemite ambitions and represented a potential source of markets, capital, and an outlet to the sea. Moreover, Jerusalem had long carried a special significance for Abdullah as a descendant of the Hashemites, family of the Prophet Muhammad. As early as 1921 he had tried to persuade Churchill that Palestine should be included in the emirate proposed for him.[23] In fact, of all the leaders of the surrounding states, Abdullah continued to take the greatest interest in Palestine.

Although for the next decade Abdullah was preoccupied with establishing his control in Transjordan, his thoughts never strayed far from Palestine or from the possibility of convincing both the Zionists and Palestinians that under his leadership they could realize their respective ambitions. In this context Abdullah's contacts with the Jews can be explained. And, as Uriel Dann points out, Abdullah, who had received his education at the center of the Ottoman Empire, saw the Jews, as the Ottomans had perceived them, as a modern *millet*, whose talents in trade and business could be exploited for his own purposes.[24] Given this approach, Abdullah's willingness to lease state lands in the Jordan valley to the Zionists makes a great deal of sense.[25]

As events in Palestine began to boil during the 1930s, Abdullah saw possibilities for carving out a larger role for himself. Generally he sought to increase his influence with the three major parties to the conflict – the Jews, the British, and Palestinians. And circumstances often played into his hands. Bitter divisions among the Palestinian Arabs gave him an opening, as opponents of the Mufti of Jerusalem Haj Amin al-Husayni looked to Amman for support. This was particularly true of the moderate pro-British Nashashibi family, who saw in Abdullah an ally to bolster their own influence inside and outside of Palestine.[26] Abdullah's tacit endorsement of the 1937 partition plan, or at least the portion endorsing the creation of an Arab state, also enhanced his reputation among the Zionists and British as a responsible and pragmatic Arab leader. Still, the failure of the partition idea and the beginning of World War II meant that Abdullah would have to cool his ambitions and wait for a more propitious moment to advance his claims.[27]

By 1947 it appeared that Abdullah might get his chance. By then, too, he had probably dropped any real hope of realizing a Greater Syria scheme and had redirected his energy toward a less elusive prize. The king did not welcome the gathering storm across the river, but he saw in the unworkability of the British mandate and London's decision in the spring of 1947 to return the Palestine issue to the United Nations an opportunity to achieve his goal of including the territory designated for an Arab state within his own kingdom. The day after the state of Israel was declared in May 1948, Jordanian forces entered the West Bank and were deployed between Nablus and Hebron. At the war's end Abdullah had added 2,200 square miles of territory to his kingdom. He had also captured Jerusalem – a prize that he believed further enhanced his personal authority and prestige.

For the next three years, until his assassination in 1951 by an embittered Palestinian nationalist, Abdullah devoted much of his energy to formalizing this control over the West Bank and trying to legitimize his acquisition in the eyes of the Arabs, Palestinians, and Israelis. First, he sought to create a new administrative and political structure in the area and to co-opt and suppress independent Palestinian nationalist activity. At the same time, in an effort to counter Egypt's attempt to institutionalize its own hold over Palestinians by creating a "Government of all-Palestine" in Gaza, Abdullah hosted Palestinian conferences in Jerusalem and later in Jericho. The latter conference called for the immediate union of the two banks under Abdullah as king. By 1950, Abdullah had forbade the use of the term Palestine in official documents and in April formally annexed the West Bank.[28] In his speech to the Parliament after the annexation, Abdullah laid out the theme of unity that was to govern the Hashemite view of the West Bank for the next four decades. "Jordan is like a bird with its wings spread east and west; it is its natural right to be united into a whole and for its people to join each other."[29] The fact that Abdullah was murdered a year later while en route to Friday prayers in East Jerusalem at the al-Aqsa mosque by a Palestinian nationalist related to the Mufti reflected both the tensions and closeness that the Hashemite relationship with Palestine had engendered.

Although Abdullah's Palestine policy created enormous problems for Jordan by incorporating hundreds of thousands of more urbanized and better educated Palestinian Arabs into a more traditional and rural East Bank environment, Abdullah believed that the war and annexation of the West Bank had strengthened his military power and political prestige. While Palestinian nationalists and a number of Arab states, led by Egypt, branded him a traitor and renegade for pursuing his own goals in Palestine, Abdullah believed that the Hashemite role there was vital to his survival. He saw his actions as a moderating buffer against the forces of Palestinian radicalism represented by the Mufti. "The Mufti and Kuwatly want to set up an independent Arab state in Palestine with the Mufti at its head. If that were to happen I would be encircled on almost all sides by enemies," he remarked to a Palestinian friend in 1947.[30] To Abdullah, the proximity of the West Bank, his ongoing rivalries with Egypt and Syria, and his own feeling of isolation and vulnerability in the Arab world demanded that he play an activist role in Palestinian affairs.

That Abdullah and later Hussein had calculated political and security objectives in Palestine is beyond dispute. Yet these should not diminish the more subjective but inextricably related factors of prestige and ideology that attracted both kings to the Palestinian cause. For Abdullah, taken with a vision of unity in which the Hashemites would play the preeminent role, Palestine was initially a stepping stone to greater things. Abdullah had never given up his quest for his elusive Syrian kingdom that he believed was destined for Hashemite control. "We, the Hashemites, left the Hijaz for the sake of Syria and Palestine," Abdullah wrote.[31] And never really content with what he described as his "wilderness of Transjordania," he looked to the outside for a grander and more fitting role to play. Although the Palestine issue complicated his relations with his Arab neighbors and indirectly linked him in negative ways with the British and the Zionists, it also gave him a vehicle to assert his traditional belief in the Hashemites' destiny and responsibility in the Arab and Muslim world.

It is important to understand Abdullah's view of his role to make sense of his policies. The bonds he felt to his family and his father, the sharif of Mecca, created a legacy that compelled him to act, and, despite his pragmatism, to follow a vision that he never had the resources to achieve. As a Hashemite, a direct descendant of the Prophet Muhammad, and son of the sharif of Mecca, Abdullah had a strong sense of his family's historic role. Moreover, as Abdullah recounted again and again, the Hashemites led the great Arab revolt during World War I and gave the Arabs national identity and spirit. He believed this legacy gave him the responsibility and duty to lay claim to the political and even religious leadership of the Arabs. In this respect Abdullah was perhaps too taken with his origins and too insistent that others recognize his importance. As Abdullah informed the Syrian prime minister,

> we of the Hashemite house were the prime factor in the Arabs' attainment to a place of honour. Their first age

of glory was the creation of Muhammed . . . and their
second was the work of the creator of the Arab Revolt.
It is because of this that some of you have become
kings, princes, and presidents and have attained other
high offices.[32]

This sense of responsibility and mission became even more
important to Abdullah after the deaths of his father Hussein
in 1931 and his elder brother Ali in 1935 made him head of
the household.[33]

Nowhere is this commitment clearer than in Abdullah's
view of Jerusalem and its importance to furthering Hashemite prestige. Thrown out of Mecca, Medina, and Damascus,
Abdullah continued to hope that the Hashemites could bring
one of the Arab world's historic cities under their control.
Jerusalem was of relatively minor political importance but
had enormous significance in religious terms. The importance
of the city, third in rank according to the holiness of its
mosques, was of no small significance to a man seeking a
regional role in an Arab and Muslim world. As early as 1934
Abdullah had written to the British high commissioner for
Palestine introducing himself as a "Muslim and a descendant
of the Prophet who is near to the Holy Places of Palestine
and particularly its Masjid al-Aqsa [al-Aqsa mosque], as a
leader who bears not a small share of responsibility for the
Arab revolt."[34] Moreover, in comparison with Amman, then
a city of some 50 thousand, Jerusalem, with a population of
160 thousand, was relatively cosmopolitan. The fact that Abdullah's father was buried in the Dome of the Rock also
enhanced the city's importance. After 1948 Abdullah, who
had himself crowned king of Jerusalem by the Coptic Church,
treated the city as a second capital and held Friday prayers
there.[35]

Thus, involvement in the Palestinian cause was partly
a natural extension of Abdullah's unique conception of the
Hashemite heritage. Equally important was that this commitment gave Abdullah and Hussein—as outsiders in an
Arab world inhabited by leaders who in turn were seeking

their own sources of legitimacy to justify their claims to power – a unique mission and destiny. Pushed out of the Arabian Peninsula by the Saudis, forced to abdicate their traditional role as protector of Mecca and Medina, and frustrated by the obstacles in the path of a Greater Syria, Abdullah saw in Palestine a way to realize the Hashemite conception of Arab unity, albeit on a smaller scale, and to acquire the prestige and status that he believed the family deserved. As T. E. Lawrence recalled, "His object was, of course, the winning of Arab independence and the building up of Arab nations, but he meant to keep the direction of the new states in the family.[36] The bitter irony of Abdullah's quest was that it brought him into direct conflict with his Arab neighbors who, paradoxically, accused him of being the only Arab to benefit from the Palestinian and Arab defeat of 1948. To make matters worse, Abdullah, and later Hussein, were portrayed as cooperating with the enemies of the Arab nation – the British, the Zionists, and the Americans. The tension between this Hashemite imperative and pressures from surrounding Arab states remains unresolved to this day.

The issue of Abdullah's relationship with the British, and, for that matter, Jordan's ties with the West, are also important factors in trying to evaluate Hashemite involvement in Palestine. Unlike Egypt or Syria, Jordan was spared much of the bitter anti-Western sentiment that the Arab national struggle for independence left in its wake. The Hashemites did their fair share of railing against the West and imperialism's plots to divide the Arab nation. But they were on far shakier ground than their Egyptian or Syrian nationalist compatriots. As Abdullah well recognized, Transjordan's creation was a direct result of one of those imperial gambits, and no amount of rhetoric about Greater Syria and restoring the unity of the Arab nation could change this fact. Moreover, Abdullah's dependence on British financial and military aid and the pro-British orientation he imparted to Hussein reinforced this bond with the West and simultaneously created a unique advantage and liability. The Hashemites were forced to operate in an Arab world in which legitimate grievances against the Europeans and baiting the West were effective ways to rally public opinion and compete for influence in the Arab arena.

What complicated matters further was Abdullah's role in the 1948 war and his highly pragmatic views of Zionism and Israel. During this period, Abdullah for the second time in 25 years managed to acquire another piece of the Palestine mandate – an act that was viewed by his Arab brothers as a betrayal of the Palestinian and Arab cause. Although the Arab Legion acquitted itself favorably, and Jerusalem and the West Bank were annexed, Abdullah was perceived as the only Arab leader to have really benefited from the war. His contacts with the Zionists both before and after the defeat only heightened the perception that the Hashemites were colluding with the British and the Jews.

Hussein, following in the traditions set by his grandfather, maintained both a pro-Western orientation and a pragmatic view of Israel. Hussein was educated at Harrow and Sandhurst, where he acquired a special affinity for the British. Despite the anti-Western sentiments that swept the Arab world during the 1950s and 1960s in the wake of the Baghdad Pact and Suez war, Hussein was able to juggle the problems of maintaining close ties to the West, guarding Jordan's independence and countering the forces of radical Arab nationalism that swirled around him. Indeed, the April 1957 Egyptian and Syrian-backed coup against him only reinforced his ties to the West and initiated a new bond with the United States, which began to play a greater role in supporting the king.

Nonetheless, Jordan's traditional alignment, first with the British and then with the United States, placed it in a very difficult position with its Arab neighbors and with respect to the Palestine problem. To the extent Jordan was identified with the United States, it had to handle the political fallout that derived from U.S. support of Israel – a problem that also dogged the Egyptians, particularly after Sadat's decision to seek U.S. aid. In this respect, Hussein jealously guards Jordan's independence on issues from arms sales to the Palestinian problem. Here Hussein has had to demonstrate, on one hand, that he is a moderate interested in a negotiated settlement, and, on the other, that he will not compromise Palestinian or Arab rights. His autumn 1985 call for direct negotiations with Israel under the auspices of an international conference is an effort to find such a middle ground.

Abdullah bequeathed a complex legacy to his grandson. Accompanying the prestige and authority Abdullah believed the West Bank had given the Hashemites was the increasingly difficult challenge of reconciling Hashemite and Palestinian interests within the context of the merged banks. For the most part Hussein followed the precedents set by his grandfather for whom he felt a deep affection and respect. Abdullah, Hussein recounts in his memoirs, had the most "profound" influence on his life.[37] The young king's view of Hashemite capabilities and regional strategy was much less pretentious than Abdullah's. Nonetheless, he subscribed to the same general view of the West Bank and to the important role the Hashemites were destined to play there.

Hussein, like Abdullah, saw some form of unity of the two banks as a natural and inevitable result of the linkage of destinies between Palestinians and Hashemites. And like Abdullah, Hussein tried through co-optation and control to subordinate a separate Palestinian identity within a larger Jordanian framework. In addition to coercion and material benefits, Hussein's secret weapon was his ability, at least until the 1960s, to manipulate Palestinian political desires and to convince the Palestinians that Arab unity under a Hashemite aegis was the most effective way to realize their joint goals of liberating Palestine.[38] "Jordanians on both Banks are equal members of one big family," Hussein remarked in April 1964.[39]

Thus, Hussein was indeed Abdullah's ideological heir. After all, Hussein reminds us in his introduction to Abdullah's memoirs, the Hashemites were standard-bearers of the Arab revolt, "the first truly Arab thrust towards achieving their liberation, unity and progress in modern times."[40] Was it not logical then that the Hashemites should also play a central role in furthering the cause of Palestine? Hussein's sense

of personal and family responsibility is an important con-
sideration in understanding Jordanian policies toward this
issue. "Jordan, and with it my family," Hussein declared
before the seventeenth session of the Palestine National
Council in Amman in November 1984, "have more than and
before anyone else stood by the Palestinian people in confronting the Zionist danger in the early days just as we are confronting it today while it is at its peak."[41]

The merging of the two identities became even more important for Hussein as the Palestinian national movement
became more independent and militant during the 1960s. The
creation of the PLO and its emphasis on a separate Palestinian entity not only challenged the Hashemites' credentials
and authority as patrons of the Palestinian cause but threatened their security. It was bad enough that Fatah and the
other independent PLO groups talked about the immediate
liberation of their land. But these nationalists also provided
a new focus of identity for Palestinians residing on the East
Bank as well. Indeed, Abdullah's worst fears about the Mufti
paled by comparison with the potential danger an independent and militant PLO would pose to his grandson.

Hussein's fateful decision to enter the 1967 war against
Israel accelerated his competition with the Palestinian movement while adding a new dimension to the Hashemite legacy
on Palestine. The war interestingly enough had one unfore-
seen benefit. Paradoxically, in defeat the Hashemites were
able to do something they were never really able to do in
victory — create closer ties with other Arab regimes such as
Egypt, which were also linked to the 1967 debacle. Nonetheless, Israel's crushing defeat of the combined Arab armies
created formidable challenges for the Hashemites. First, it
strengthened the prestige and power of independent Palestinian organizations and increased their ability to compete with
Hussein and other Arab leaders for leadership on the Palestinian issue. Moreover, Israel's crackdown on Palestinian activity in the West Bank led the fedayeen to shift the focus
of their activities to the East Bank, setting the stage for the
events of September 1970. Second, the consequences of the
defeat, despite the Jordanian army's relatively credible show-

ing, was a terrible blow personally to Hussein and to Hashemite authority. Hashemites who had taken Jerusalem and the West Bank a decade and half earlier were now burdened with its loss. "My brothers, I seem to belong to a family which, according to the will of Allah, must suffer and make sacrifices for the country without end," Hussein announced over Radio Amman on June 7.[42] The Hashemites in Jordan, who alone among the sons of Sharif Hussein had acquired and maintained a throne, were now humiliated and again associated with the loss of yet another holy city. For Hussein, the loss of Jerusalem and the West Bank only intensified his desire to regain the legacy that he believed it was his duty to protect. Accepting this loss would have been tantamount to abandoning the heritage he had received from his family and to "renouncing a mission" he was not entitled to forsake.[43]

As I pointed out before, the Hashemite interest in the West Bank went beyond matters of prestige and focused on the authority and survival of the regimes. The Abdullah-Mufti rivalry was now replaced by a more bitter struggle between Hussein and Arafat, culminating in the explosive events of Black September 1970. If the king had any doubts that the Palestinian question could engulf both banks of the Jordan River, they were shattered by the fedayeen challenge to his authority. After 1970, Hussein became even more determined to defuse, co-opt, and manage the forces of Palestinian nationalism.

Once again, hard political and demographic realities only confirmed the Hashemite view that Jordanian-Palestinian destinies had to be linked within a common but Hashemite-dominated framework. And it was no coincidence that within a year after the Jordanian army had defeated the remaining Palestinian forces at Ajlun, Hussein floated his March 1972 plan for a Federated Arab Kingdom consisting of two regions, one on each side of the river with one army, federal judiciary, and executive controlled by Amman. The West Bank's capital was to be Jerusalem and it was to have its own judiciary, executive, and legislative authority within the federal structure.

Although the Rabat decision of October–November 1974 undercut Hussein's role and elevated the PLO to an unprecedented level of authority, he continued to emphasize the importance of a confederal relationship. In May 1982 he noted, "we and the Palestinians have been a single people in the past and the present . . . this future may be realized in a declaration of a federation (union) between the West Bank and Jordan on the basis of Jordanian and Palestinian choice."[44] The Reagan initiative in September 1982, the ongoing dialogue with Arafat, the Palestine National Council 1984 meeting, and the February 1985 Jordanian-Palestinian agreement has kept the issue of a confederal framework on center stage.

Nowhere is Hussein's conception of Jordan's involvement in the Palestinian question and his thoughts on the nature of the Jordanian-Palestinian relationship better revealed than in his speech before the seventeenth session of the Palestine National Council meeting. The address is significant for many reasons, not the least of which was Hussein's opportunity to speak directly, in a forum sanctioned by the PLO, to Palestinians in the diaspora and on the West Bank. Thus, it presented the king with a rare opportunity to outline Jordan's views on the past and future dimensions of its Palestinian policy.[45]

The speech consists of two basic parts. First, the king examined the nature of Jordan's relationship with the Palestinian issue during the last half century in an effort to demonstrate how intimate the relationship has been and how much Jordan has sacrificed. These sacrifices are not only Jordanian but Hashemite. The symbolism is striking. Sharif Hussein, the king points out, sacrificed his throne in defense of Palestine by refusing to sign a treaty with Britain until it revoked the Balfour Declaration; Abdullah sacrificed his life in his "sincere effort to save the biggest part of Palestine." The tone of the remarks were cast, not surprisingly, in terms of an ideological and moral commitment on behalf of the Palestinian cause. "You can see from the historical facts," Hussein informed the delegates, "that we as a Hashemite family have never disavowed, God forbid, the Palestinian identity and aspirations or tried to dominate Palestine and its people." It is striking how much of the speech focused on this Hashemite commitment.

Much the same tone was brought to the second part of the address in which Hussein focused on the future of the relationship. The king earlier describes the convening of the Palestine National Council as a "natural return to what should and would continue to be" the nature of a special relationship between Jordan and Palestine. Interestingly enough, Hussein portrayed what he calls "objective" or "scientific" facts such as geography, history, and demography to prove how close the relationship must be. In fact, it is partly these objective factors that have bound the "two fraternal peoples and countries" since the turn of the century in the "same boat of suffering, hope, interest, harm, history, and destiny." The Islamic and Arab dimension of the relationship is never far behind. "Palestine embraces Jerusalem, the cradle of Jesus . . . the place from which Muhammed . . . ascended to the heavens; . . . the battlefield of Salah al-Din; the resting place of Husayn ibn 'Ali; and the martyr's ladder to glory."

Although Hussein has tempered Abdullah's plans to assert full sovereignty over both banks of the Jordan and has come to accept the need for the fulfillment of separate Palestinian national aspirations, the legacy of Abdullah still weighs heavily upon him. And the idea that Jordanians and Palestinians are one family and that the two banks should be united under the beneficent patronage of the Hashemites, remains a powerful force in the king's calculations. "I am not a West Banker and I cannot speak for them," Hussein once noted, "but my own family has been linked to Palestinian rights since the beginning of this century."[46] These factors of prestige, duty, and personal and family responsibility explain much about the Hashemite involvement in the affairs of Palestine. It may well be, however, that the same responsibilities and duties that have defined Jordan's involvement in the West Bank and Hussein's view that he cannot satisfactorily discharge them without exposing himself to serious political risks, ultimately will prevent him from accomplishing his objectives west of the Jordan River.

# 4

# Syria and the Palestinian Cause: Touchstone of Arab Nationalism

You should not forget that Syria is the cradle of Arab Nationalism. We have never capitulated from the days of the Crusaders to modern Zionist expansionism.[47]
— Hafiz al-Assad

For Syria, like Jordan, the Palestinian issue has been deeply rooted in its history, politics, and geography for more than half a century. These factors have created an important role for Syria to play and have linked the Palestinian cause to contemporary Syrian politics and to the legitimacy of various Syrian regimes in important ways. Involvement in the affairs of Palestine and, by implication, in the confrontation with Zionism and Israel is not only a political lever routinely pulled by aspiring Syrian politicians or an intellectual abstraction tossed about by Ba'thi ideologues. It cuts to the core of Syria's self-image as the cradle of Arab nationalism and is linked to managing the current challenges confronting a minority Alawite regime attempting to legitimize itself at home while acquiring the prestige in the region it deems vital to its security and survival.

That Syria's conception of its role may be grandiose and out of proportion to its capabilities does not mean it is not sincerely held. Indeed, the pragmatism that has characterized

Syrian policies since the rise of Assad should not obscure Syria's strong commitment to Arab nationalism, Arab unity, and the Palestinian cause. Although pan-Arabism in the literal Nasserist or Ba'thist sense is a relic of the past, Syria has staked out for itself a more manageable but ambitious Arab mission in what could be called the Lebanese-Jordanian-Palestinian arena. It is in this area – not coincidentally an arena in which a good part of the Arab-Israeli conflict will be decided – that Syria seeks to play a preeminent role. That pan-Arab role is not predicated upon institutional or geographic mergers but on creating a sphere of influence that forces these states and the PLO to respect Syrian security and political interests and defer to Damascus on major decisions in the Arab-Israeli arena. Championship and control of the Palestinian cause is a vital component of Syria's self-imposed sense of mission, and Assad is determined to shape the Arab agenda on this issue.

Syria's commitment to Arab unity and the Palestinian cause, however, goes beyond an idealized sense of duty and historical mission and flows from the Ba'thi view of power and its relationship to the Arab-Israeli conflict, as well as Syria's role in the international system. And under Assad, the most pragmatic of all Ba'thi leaders, these values play a major role in shaping Syrian tactics and strategy in what Damascus perceives to be an extremely risky and dangerous game. Assad has long believed that the Arabs must deal with Israel from a position of political and military parity. Although he knows this may not be possible in the short term, Syria must at least prevent states such as Lebanon and Jordan from settling with Israel and irrevocably shifting the political balance of power against Syria. Allowing other Arab states to cut separate deals with Israel to regain their territory, let alone move toward a resolution of the Palestinian problem, not only compromises Syria's ability to regain the Golan Heights but might ultimately compromise the authority of a regime that has prided itself on its role as the preeminent confrontation state and guardian of Arab rights and honor. This role, undertaken by a minority Alawite Ba'thi regime in a predominantly Sunni Muslim society, is a central element in Assad's effort to create a sense of Syrian national identity that transcends sectarian affiliation.

It is precisely for these reasons that Syria has vociferously opposed and tried to undermine the Camp David and the Israeli-Lebanese May 17 accords — both, from Syria's perspective, U.S.-brokered efforts to cut separate deals between Israel and two "confrontation states" — one of which is in Syria's own backyard. Moreover, Syria will oppose any effort to resolve the Palestinian problem that ignores its territorial interests on the Golan and does not allow it a preeminent role in championing the Palestinian cause. The importance Syria attached to the Palestinian issue increased dramatically after Sadat proved to the Arab world that negotiations with Israel could lead to the return of Arab territory. Although Syria could tolerate an Egyptian-Israeli deal on Sinai and deride it as a separate sell out, it cannot allow a resolution of the Palestinian problem based on a Jordanian option, in which a Palestinian entity falls under the influence of the Jordanian regime and tacitly under Israeli influence as well. Such a solution would reduce Syria's own importance in the Arab arena and increase its isolation.

As with the Hashemites, the origins of Syria's relationship to the Palestinian cause predates the modern history of the Syrian state. In Syria's case, however, the issue is even more intertwined in the images and perceptions of a distant past. For more than a thousand years from the end of the Umayyad Caliphate in the eighth century to the first half of the twentieth century, there was no independent Syria. The area that now constitutes Syria had been part of the Ottoman Empire since the sixteenth century. In fact, the *vilayet* (province) of Syria encompassed all of what was Palestine, Transjordan, and Lebanon until the mid-nineteenth century — a fact that would only reinforce the Syrian view that these territories were organic parts of the Syrian whole.

An independent and irredentist Syria was not to remain submerged for long. In the aftermath of World War I, Syria was caught up in the crosscurrents of the tumultuous search for Arab unity and independence that swept the region. It is here in the mix of past and present – so vital to understanding Syria's worldview – that the roots of Syria's modern identity began to crystallize. Syria remained more an object of these forces than an active initiator.[48] But it was clear even then that Syria was destined to play an important role in the region. The area was strategically located astride the northeastern approaches to the Nile Valley and was an overland link between the Mediterranean and the Persian Gulf.[49] Moreover, the area was the historic seat of the Umayyad Caliphate – a period in which Arab prestige and consciousness were at their peak. Both of these factors made Syria an important prize for those Arab nationalists who sought to capitalize on its role in Arab and Islamic history. And it was no coincidence that the final act in the great Arab Revolt and efforts to establish Faisal as an Arab king were played out in Damascus.

Political reasons also focused this renewed Arab nationalist activity in Syria. By the nineteenth century, the province of Syria, the largest of the Ottoman *vilayets*, was already the scene of anti-Turkish agitation and reaction against the increasingly authoritarian policies of Sultan Abdul Hamid II. Even earlier, the British consul at Aleppo, in one of the earliest indications of anti-Turkish semtiment, wrote, "It would also appear that the Mussulman population of Northern Syria harbours hopes of a separation from the Ottoman Empire and the formation of a new Arab State under the sovereignty of the Shereefs of Mecca. . . . "[50] The consul was doubtless exaggerating the motives of a movement that was based as late as 1915 on the importance of reform within the Ottoman system rather than separation from it.[51]

During the war years, however, the harshness of Turkish occupation policies in Syria further galvanized this inchoate nationalist activity and forced a growing number of Arab nationalists to think more in terms of separation from the Ottoman Empire. Syria was to be the focus of these efforts. Egged on by British promises and blinded by their own ambitions, the sons of the sharif of Mecca, indeed Sharif Hussein himself, believed that at the war's end an Arab kingdom would be established that would include at least a part of Syria, including Damascus, Homs, Hama, and Aleppo. And for a short while their expectations were fulfilled. On September 30, 1918, 400 years of Turkish rule symbolically came to an end, not in Cairo, Beirut, Baghdad, or Jerusalem but in Damascus, where the Arab flag of King Hussein of the Hijaz was hoisted over the town hall.[52]

It was not the Turks, however, who were destined to provide the real impetus for the resurgence of Arab nationalism and create the role Syria would define for itself in the Arab renaissance. The formal disintegration of the Ottoman state left a vacuum that the British and French sought to fill. The Sykes-Picot agreement, the Balfour Declaration, and the mandate system inevitably led to a confrontation with these emerging national movements and thwarted Arab ambitions and frustrated wartime hopes. Once again, Syria was the stage on which the postwar drama unfolded. An Arab army occupied Damascus, an Arab king with religious and political authority was prepared to assume power, and an Arab National Congress enacted a nationalist program. From 1918 to 1920, Arabism became the dominant ideology in Syria, and no political personality of any stature could oppose it.[53]

If the hopes and illusions were all the greater in Syria, then so was the eventual disappointment. Within 20 months of his installation, Faisal was ejected from Damascus, and within two years a French mandate was instituted that left a legacy of suspicion, resentment, and bitterness that characterizes Syrian policies toward the West to this day. Moreover, within two decades, the Syrian nationalists saw their patrimony systematically stripped and dismembered by what they believed to be an imperialist and Zionist conspiracy. Lebanon went to France; Transjordan to the Hashemites and British; Alexandretta to the Turks; and finally in 1917, 1948, and, again, in 1967, parts of Palestine to the Zionists.[54] The notion that the West, with Israeli support, is still determined to divide the Arab nation is a vital component of the Syrian worldview.

It is in the context of this emerging anti-imperialist, nationalist, and anti-Zionist mix that Syria's commitment to the Palestinian issue was initially formed. The view that the West was assaulting Syria's geographic and political identity left an enduring mark on Syria's political consciousness. In 1919, shortly after the announcement of the French mandate for Syria, the Syrian cabinet, in presenting its program to the National Congress, proclaimed its aims, one of which was "to stand for the unity of Syria within its natural boundaries" and rejected the Zionist claim to transform a part of southern Syria (Palestine) into a Jewish national home.[55] And it is no coincidence that Palestinian Arabs identifying with this Syrian nationalist movement sent delegations to both National Congresses of 1919 and 1920.[56] Paradoxically, Faisal, like his brother Abdullah, took a remarkably pragmatic view of the possibilities of cooperating with the Zionists. With his ouster and the beginnings of the French mandate, any flexibility, however, was lost amidst the escalating anti-Zionist and anti-Western sentiments of many of the nationalists.

For the next two decades, Syrians turned inward, preoccupied with their nationalist struggle against the French. The mandate provided a powerful catalyst for the formulation of an intensely anti-Western and anti-Zionist ideology and imparted to Syria a bitter irredentist foreign policy orientation as the French pursued what has been described as a "self-interested policy of division and exploitation."[57] Hardened by the loss of Palestine and Transjordan, during these early years the nationalists saw the source of their problems in Western imperialism and the source of their salvation in Arab unity.

Nowhere did this Western conspiracy seem clearer than across Syria's southwestern border. Throughout the years of French rule, Syrian interest in Palestine remained high. Violent demonstrations were staged against Lord Balfour when he visited Damascus in 1925. And both the 1929 riots and the 1936 Arab rebellion heightened pan-Arab feeling as Syrian nationalists saw struggle against the Zionists and British as part of the eventual liberation of all of historic

Syria. One of the preeminent military figures in the Arab Revolt, Fawzi al-Qawuqji, was a Syrian, and exiled Palestinian leaders used Syria as their base.[58] And in 1937 in Bludan near the Lebanese-Syrian border, an inter-Arab conference was convened to discuss the Arab response to the revolt. Throughout the 1940s, Syria participated in Arab conferences on Palestine and joined the newly created Arab League in 1945.[59]

The creation of Israel and the first Arab-Israeli war, however, provided the major turning point in Syrian involvement in the Palestine issue and linked the problem irrevocably to internal Syrian politics and foreign policy. That the consequences of the Arab defeat in Palestine first registered in Syria should come as no surprise. The Syrians, always first to proclaim their commitment to the Arab nationalist cause, invested heavily in the war, and expectations of success were extraordinarily high. Not only were Syrian regular army units, equipped with armor and artillery, involved along the northern front, but Qawuqji led irregular forces into battle. Within two weeks of the Arab intervention, the weakness and ineptitude of the army's performance became clear.[60] The military's role soon led to domestic political tensions as a younger generation of army officers began to blame traditional politicians and even their own commanders for the military debacle. Because the army was held in such high regard as one of the finest Syrian institutions, particularly after independence in 1946, the magnitude of defeat was even greater. The war discredited the upper-class nationalists and polarized relations between the military and civilian elite. It also energized new parties such as the Ba'th, which began to use the Palestine issue to promote the need for Arab unity and social change.[61]

In March 1949, army Commander in Chief Husni Za'im seized power in a bloodless coup touched off by a wide range of popular grievances, particularly accusations that the politicians had provided poor support for Syrian units fighting in Palestine. The Za'im coup, the first successful army coup in the Arab world, not only revealed how important the Pales-

tine issue would become in Syrian politics but demonstrated
to a new generation of Syrian leaders how valuable the military was as an agent for change. In fact, much of the support for the Za'im coup came from the Ba'this, who believed
that a military government could open up a new era in Syria,
produce a strong national identity, and carry on the struggle for Arab unity, socialism, and the war against Zionism.

For the next decade and a half, Syria again turned inward, caught between a fragmented and unstable internal
situation and the rise of Nasser's Egypt and its emerging con-
test with Israel and the West. Syria was in no condition to
assert itself into the emerging pan-Arab currents. By the end
of 1949, Damascus had witnessed three military coups. A
fourth brought to power a military dictatorship that ended
in 1954. By 1958, in an effort to check the growing influence
of the Communists and with the support of the Ba'th Party,
which increasingly looked to Egypt as the best vehicle to at-
tain Arab unity, the regime pushed for union with Egypt. The
United Arab Republic, based on little more than a temporary
coincidence of interests and the illusion of Arab unity, collapsed three years later, paving the way for the March 1963
coup and the emergence of the Ba'th Party as the preeminent
force in Syrian politics.

The Ba'th's rise marked another major turning point in
Syria's relationship with the Palestinian issue and brought
to power a party that was committed in principle and in practice to Arab unity and the Palestinian cause. No Ba'thi leader
would allow pan-Arabism or Palestine to jeopardize the regime's interests, however. And by 1970 with the emergence
of Hafiz al-Assad, a pragmatist even by Ba'thi standards, the
emphasis was on promoting more defined Syrian as opposed
to pan-Arab interests. Nonetheless, the Ba'th Party established the outline of Syrian foreign policy and cast it in an
activist and irredentist mode. That Syria had abandoned, in
any practical sense, the idea of institutionalized mergers with
Lebanon, Jordan, or Palestine should not diminish the importance the Ba'th attached to playing a preeminent role in
these areas. Moreover, the need for an increasingly Alawite-

dominated regime to maintain its legitimacy and prestige at home required assertive and bold policies in the inter-Arab and Arab-Israeli arenas. In short, Syria was in search of an Arab role to play based on the rather simple assumption that what was good for Syria — cradle of Arabism and home of the Ba'th Party — would be good for the "Arab nation." Nowhere would this become clearer than in Syria's need to champion and control the Palestinian cause.

Ba'thi interest and involvement in the Palestine issue derived from its relationship to Arabism. In fact, two of the three salient elements in Ba'thist ideology — Arab unity and independence — are encapsulated in the Palestinian question. Interestingly enough, a third, socialism, is also linked to the Palestine issue. Only when the political order could be better harmonized and the tensions between classes and communal groups resolved could the strength of the Arab nations be restored for the struggle against Zionism. The Ba'this had long believed it was the weakness and corruption of the old regimes that had produced the defeat of 1948. The defeat in 1948 was the "bell toll for the 'bankrupt' Arab governments and it ushered in a new era — an era of revolution," wrote Munif al-Razzaz, Michel Aflaq's successor as secretary general of the Ba'th Party.[62] And the road to Arab unity, as Aflaq himself had written, lay through Palestine.

Once in power, the Ba'th, particularly after civilian militants had consolidated their control in 1966, went beyond mere sloganeering on this issue. From 1966 onward, the commitment to Palestine became an active and vital component of Syrian policy.[63] Ideology and self-interest merged in a dynamic conception of Syrian interests. Both became mixed in an anti-imperialist and anti-Zionist mind-set that affected domestic and foreign policy issues. The more militant regionalists within the party, who sought to take control from the old guard Ba'thists, attacked the old guard's willingness to defer to Nasser's support for summit conferences rather than on armed struggle.[64] And Syria, which had supported Fatah's activities since the late 1950s, began to increase its assistance to fedayeen groups to counter Nasser's support for the PLO.

A war of popular liberation had a certain appeal to Ba'thi ideologues as Damascus actively promoted Palestinian raids through Jordan into Israel. Support for the fedayeen, although curtailed when the Syrians believed it to be in their interests, became the "touchstone" for promoting Arabism and continuing the conflict with Israel, and fedayeen activity played an important role in escalating tensions along the Syrian-Israeli border and in setting the stage for the 1967 war.

The debacle of 1967 made the Palestinian issue and Syria's need to play the role of confrontation state even more important. The loss of the Golan Heights and Syria's poor performance in the war did not sober the Ba'thi view of the conflict. Syria was suspicious of the emerging Egyptian-Jordanian axis and was the only Arab country to boycott the Khartoum conference in 1967, which it described as the "latest podium for the advocates of the liquidation of the Palestine cause."[65] Damascus, unlike Cairo or Amman, which began to explore the possibility of using political means to regain their lost territory, resisted any nonmilitary solution to the Arab-Israeli conflict. In fact the tenth Ba'th Party Congress in March 1970 was highly significant in this regard — condemning any "deviationist tendencies" and "opportunist outlook" that might compel other Arab states to seek a separate settlement of the Palestinian issue.[66] As internal rivalries between the civilian wing of the Ba'th Party under Salah Jadid and its military wing led by Hafiz al-Assad began to intensify, the Palestinian issue assumed an even greater importance. In an effort to counter the military's forces and to demonstrate their own commitment to the Palestinian cause, the Jadidists created their own Palestinian organization, Sa'iqa.

It is striking that the event that triggered the final showdown within the Ba'th Party and led to the Assad coup of November 1970 was Syria's decision to support the fedayeen's challenge to King Hussein in September. Assad, then chief of the air force, did not oppose the intervention of Syrian-backed Palestinian Liberation Army tanks in Jordan, but he was wary of triggering an Israeli or even a U.S. reaction and thus opposed the use of Syrian air support. Assad's reaction to the Jordanian crisis reflected the new pragmatism that he would bring to Syrian foreign policy. The new flexibility was based on Assad's belief that Syria could not pursue its goals from an isolated position within the Arab world or by allowing the fedayeen the kind of independence that could destabilize Arab regimes or drag the Syrians into an unwanted or untimely war with Israel. Similarly, the future Syrian president saw the limitations of a popular war of liberation and began to base Syrian military strategy on a buildup of conventional military forces. Assad began to temper the revisionist enthusiasm of his more militant colleagues and brought Syria's immediate objectives more into line with its capabilities.[67] In the wake of the 1973 war, Assad negotiated a disengagement agreement with Israel and, through his acceptance of UN Security Council Resolution 338, implicitly accepted Resolution 242 — something the Ba'this had earlier vowed Syria would never do.

Nonetheless, Assad's tactical flexibility and his decision to reorient the unrealistic expectations of those Ba'thists who pushed pan-Arabism as an operational goal should not suggest that he was any less influenced by the importance of Syria's commitment to Arabism and the Palestine cause. As I indicated earlier, the salience of these values derived from the Ba'thi view of a world in which power defines relationships as well as success or failure. The key to understanding Assad and Syria and their relationship to the Palestinian issue since 1970 is this conception of power and the role it plays in the Arab-Israeli arena. Assad's pragmatism is rooted in his understanding both of the limitations under which he is operating as a result of Israel's military superiority and the strengths Syria possesses in relation to the weakness of its Arab neighbors. Assad is under no illusions about Arab unity or about Syria's ability to dominate the Arab world in any pan-Arab sense — a strategy that only evokes painful memories of failed mergers and unrealistic goals of the past. What Assad has done, however, is to stake out a preeminent position in the Palestinian-Jordanian-Lebanese triangle. To do this, he needs a unified Arab position vis-à-vis Israel that is based on tacit Lebanese, Jordanian, and PLO acceptance of Syria's view of the conflict – a view that combines Syria's national interests with elements of the broader Arab consensus.

Nowhere has Assad's determination to set the Arab agenda been more clearly evident than in his efforts to champion and control the Palestinian national movement. The importance of the Palestinian issue for Syria did not begin with the Assad era but was rooted in the Ba'thi notion of Arabism and Arab independence. Months before Assad took power the tenth Ba'th Party Conference had reaffirmed the basis from which Assad's views of the Palestinian problem would flow. The party noted that the Palestine movement was one of the focuses of the Arab revolution and that "deviationist tendencies arising from a regionalist or opportunist outlook must be crushed since it could break the dialectical relationship between the Palestinian and Arab revolutions."[68] These "deviationist tendencies" were intended to characterize the efforts of any single Arab state to depart from the Arab consensus on the Palestine issue or to weaken the "Arab nation's" ability to deal with Israel from a position of strength. This notion provided the basis of Assad's own view of the problem. It was not enough for Syria to champion the Palestinian cause, Syria had to establish itself as a guardian of Arabism to ensure that other Arab regimes and the Palestinians themselves did not violate the consensus set by the "Arab nation" on this issue.

Thus, in an effort to protect its own interests and to ensure that any final settlement to the Arab-Israeli conflict would be comprehensive, Syria assumed the role of the Arab conscience on the Palestinian issue. Much like a parent that has to discipline a wayward child, the Syrians became self-styled arbiters of what was permissible and what was forbidden. This affinity, which many pro-Syrian PLO activists were only too willing to encourage, was reinforced by geographic and historical ties. And Syrian politicians were themselves eager to make the connection. "Palestine is not only part of the Arab homeland," Assad noted on the fifteenth anniversary of the 1963 Ba'thi coup, "but is an essential part of southern Syria."[69] Or as a close Assad adviser described it,

"The Palestinian problem is a Syrian problem and an Arab problem."[70] Indeed, Syria not only sought to make Palestinian and Syrian interests synonymous but also quite naturally assumed that the PLO's objectives were subsumed under Syrian aegis. Although most Arab regimes were often forced to subordinate Palestinian interests to their own national concerns, Syria seemed to believe it had a right and responsibility to do so.

It is within this context that Syria has rationalized its violent confrontations with the PLO. And here the clash between Syrian national interests and the broader "Arab good" becomes difficult to reconcile. Both in the 1975 and 1983 clashes with the PLO in Lebanon the Syrians found themselves in the somewhat anomalous position of bashing their supposed Palestinian allies. Following the Syrian support for the Fatah mutiny in the summer of 1983 and Assad's expulsion of Yasir Arafat from Damascus, the Syrians were once again confronted with this issue and sought to provide the justification for their actions.

In July 1983, shortly after the Syrians threw Arafat out of Damascus, a two-part news analysis appeared in the influential Syrian magazine *Tishrin*.[71] The articles, entitled "Arafat and Us," were designed to counter charges that Syria was exploiting the PLO's internal troubles for its own narrow purposes. In this respect the articles provide a fascinating look into Syria's view of the relationship between Palestinian independence and the Syrian-defined Arab consensus. Throughout, the article attacked the PLO's notion of "independent Palestinian decision making" as an Arafat-inspired rationale to betray the Arab and Palestinian cause by selling out Arab interests and rights. Under the slogan of independent decision making, the magazine mockingly observes, Sadat cut a separate deal with Israel, Hussein tried to betray the PLO, and the Lebanese Phalange Party cooperated with Israel. Arafat wants "an independent decision for an independent surrender and independent forsaking of the cause." For Syria the only independent decision it will accept is the decision to "liberate the land and restore the rights." And in what is the most telling description of the Syrian view on who should establish the boundaries for Arab decision, *Tishrin* concludes:

> We will not tolerate the freedom to commit treason or to sell out the cause. Palestine is southern Syria, and whoever attacks the Palestinian organizations struggling for an independent decision in accordance with its national struggle concept will not allow such a Palestinian decision to be tampered with under the cover of any slogan or verbal screen.[72]

Thus, for Syria, the Palestinian problem is the property of the Arab nation as defined by Syria. And it is clear as the Arafat-Assad feud intensifies that Syria is prepared to defend this proposition—even at the expense of further isolation within the Arab world. As Assad declared in his speech before the opening of the eighth Ba'th Party Congress in January 1985, "Do they [the Palestinians] want to say that the Palestinian question is only theirs and not also ours. . . . How can the Palestinian question not be ours, even though we are placing all of this country's human, military, economic, and political resources at the service of this question?"[73] It does sometimes appear that Syria revels in this isolation, rationalizing that its self-styled commitment to Arabism and its willingness to oppose the "reactionary and imperialist" designs to divide the Arab nation will ultimately demonstrate to the Arabs that Syria's path remains the only course to follow. Whether Damascus succeeds, however, will depend less on its own revolutionary fervor and more on the actions of Israel and its Arab rivals. For, in the end, the real strength of Syria's Arabism is rooted not only in its military power or terrorist potential but also in its conviction that no other Arab regime and certainly no Israeli government will be able to reach an agreement on the Palestinian issue that meets Arab and Palestinian demands. Should negotiations begin without Damascus, however, the Syrians might have to redefine their own role and confront the choice of joining the negotiating process or risk being shut out entirely, thus losing any hope of regaining Syrian territory.

# 5

# Egypt and the Palestinian Cause:
# Benefit and Burden

It was Nasser who filled the Arab world, and the world
at large, with the name of Palestine.[74]

— Anwar Sadat

Unlike Jordan and Syria, Egypt lacked the powerful
demographic, historical, and territorial ties that have bound
the Hashemites and Syrians to the Palestinian issue for more
than half a century. Egypt was a relative latecomer to the
affairs of Palestine, never hosted a particularly large number
of Palestinian refugees in Egypt proper, and could not claim
that large sections of the Palestine mandate had been ar-
bitrarily carved out of its own territory. More important, a
distinct territorial identity, ethnic homogeneity, and a tradition of strong central government had given Egypt a defined
sense of national identity. Separated from the Arab east by
desert and a singular preoccupation with ending British occupation, Egypt was largely removed from the confusing and
contradictory crosscurrents out of which the mandate for
Palestine and the modern states of Syria and Jordan emerged.
While the sons of the sharif of Mecca struggled to claim the
elusive Arab kingdom promised them by Allah and the British Colonial Office, Egyptian nationalists were already nego-

tiating a treaty with London that recognized Egypt's status as an independent nation.

It is all the more ironic then that it was an Egyptian leader who played the preeminent Arab role in elevating the Palestine problem to unprecedented heights in the Arab world and identifying Egypt so closely with its resolution. It was not unusual that Gamal Abdel Nasser embraced the Palestinian issue as a way to enhance his authority at home and in the region; this was after all an elemental role to play in the Arab political game. What was striking was the powerfully convincing way Nasser played his role and the impact he would have on forcing others to embrace the issue of Palestine whether they were believers or not. In this respect, he brilliantly orchestrated the themes of Arabism and Arab independence that gave the Palestinian cause a deep resonance in the region. Even the most militant Palestinians, convinced that they themselves would eventually have to take the lead in liberating their homeland, looked to Nasser initially as the source of their salvation.

But Nasser alone, for all his appeal and his embodiment of Egyptian national and regional aspirations, could not speak for Egypt. His views of Egypt's regional and pan-Arab responsibilities and the search for hegemony and security that flowed from them were already evident in somewhat different form as early as the 1930s.[75] They coexisted, however, with other powerful imperatives and traditions rooted in Egypt's unique past. It was less a question of Egypt's ancient pharaonic roots — a theme that is often pushed to an extreme in an effort to explain Egyptian behavior — and more a result of the country's unique modern historical and political development that was responsible for its different perspective on the Palestinian issue. Egypt was larger, more homogeneous, cohesive, politically sophisticated, and secure than either Jordan or Syria, which were still under the influence of traditional leaders unsure of their own roles and identities. There were few religious or communal divisions in Egyptian society that threatened internal stability or limited the regime's foreign policy options. The Hashemites, Alawis, and Ba'this had their own particular traditions, but none appeared as secure or as fixed in time and place. While this Egyptian separateness generated a certain insecurity about Egypt's role in the Arab world and spurred Nasser to wrap himself tightly in the symbols of Arabism to promote his influence, it also created a source of confidence, strength, and pride. It is this other dimension of Egypt's political culture that allowed Nasser's successor to depart radically from an established and almost inviolate Arab consensus and to pursue Egypt's own interests after 1973.

All of these factors have allowed Egypt a greater degree of flexibility and detachment with regard to the Palestinian problem than either Jordan or Syria could afford. In both of these regimes, the Palestinian issue is so bound up with immutable factors such as history, demography, and geography that it permits them only scant room to maneuver. In Egypt, on the other hand, the Palestine issue is only one component of a political culture and social structure that predates the modern Arab-Israeli conflict by generations and, some would argue, by centuries. Over the past quarter-century, three Egyptian presidents have demonstrated a remarkable capacity to shift their approaches to this problem in a way that would probably be impossible for Syria or Jordan. Since Nasser, Egypt has been able to champion the Palestinian cause yet withdraw from the confrontation line with Israel without jeopardizing its domestic stability or permanently undermining its influence in the Arab world. This transition from Nasser's dramatic engagement on Palestine through Sadat's retrenchment to Husni Mubarak's effort to strike a balance between the two on this issue does not suggest that Egypt has no genuine commitment to the Palestinian issue. But it does indicate that Egypt's initial involvement in the affairs of Palestine was to a greater degree than elsewhere a political commitment voluntarily undertaken and fashioned by one man and his era. And it was Egypt's ability to redefine this commitment that permitted Sadat and Mubarak to reshape Nasser's vision according to their conception of Egypt's interests.

As a number of scholars have pointed out, Egypt's interest in the affairs of Palestine developed more slowly than Jordan's or Syria's.[76] Until the 1930s Egyptians were preoccupied almost exclusively with their own affairs and their relationship with the British rather than with events in the Arab and Islamic East. Despite Palestinian efforts to attract Egypt to their cause, the Egyptian public expressed little religious or political interest in the Palestine issue. Equally important and in marked contrast to the situation in Transjordan and Syria, official Egypt was also relatively disinterested in this problem. Although the 1929 riots in Jerusalem generated some concern over the fate of the Muslim holy places, neither the palace nor the government became involved. Egyptian King Fu'ad's biographer recounts that the king believed this issue to be entirely a matter for the British government.[77] And, during these early years, there appeared to be little patent connection between Egypt's interests and events in Palestine. As late as 1931 Egypt did not even send an official delegation to attend the Islamic Conference in Jerusalem.

Throughout the 1930s, Egyptian popular and official interest in the Palestine problem began to grow. The change was partly stimulated by escalating violence between Jews and Arabs in Palestine and partly by increasing Jewish immigration, which now threatened to turn the idea of a Jewish homeland into a reality. Nonetheless, these developments in Palestine would never have had much of an impact if they had not coincided with the emergence of more pan-Islamic and pan-Arab trends in Egypt itself. Under King Fu'ad's successor King Faruq, who openly encouraged both of these trends, and with the active support of groups such as the Young Men's Muslim Association and the Muslim Brotherhood, Egyptians became more attuned to the Arab and Islamic world to the east and Egypt's potential role in this arena. Indeed, writers such as Sati al-Husri argued that Egypt was uniquely endowed to play a leading role in the Arab national movement and was destined to break out of its purely Egyptian national orientation to take its rightful place in the region.[78] The views of Egyptian-firsters such as Taha Husayn were now increasingly attacked on the grounds that there was no reason that loyalty to Egypt should preclude a commitment to the Arab nation. Egypt's treaty of alliance with Britain in 1936, which formally terminated the British occupation of Egypt, allowed Cairo more independence in foreign affairs as well as an opportunity to concentrate on the Arab East. The death of Fu'ad in 1936 and the emergence of Ali Mahir, an Egyptian prime minister with a regional outlook, indicated that the way was open for a more activist role abroad.[79]

It was not surprising that the 1936 Arab revolt in Palestine markedly increased popular Egyptian interest in the Palestinian problem.[80] The revolt – the longest anticolonial rebellion in the east during the interwar period – reflected the key themes that would give the Palestinian issue such broad appeal – support for fellow Arabs and freedom from European control.[81] Moreover, the struggle was cast in both political and religious terms. Palestinian Arabs were perceived as Arabs struggling against the forces of imperialism and as Muslims combatting the "plots" and "depravity" of the Jews.[82] These sentiments found particularly fertile soil in the activities of the Muslim Brotherhood, which increased its influence and stature during this period. The events in Palestine also buoyed Egypt's own sense of struggle against the British and reinforced the growing sentiment that Egypt had a much wider role and mission to play. In fact, writers began to focus on Egypt's crucial role in countering the double threat of Zionism and imperialism in Palestine. In 1936, the famous Egyptian writer and intellectual Muhammed Hussein Heykal noted that it was necessary for every "intelligent Arab to understand that the imperialists wish to transform Palestine into a foreign land, that is, to deprive it of its Arabism and its Islam and to detach it like a piece of flesh from the Arab body."[83]

The Egyptian government could not help but be influenced by these developments and sought to use the Palestine issue to promote its own influence. Pan-Arabism and the

Palestine issue were also emerging as useful propaganda tools in the escalating struggle between Faruq and Mustafa al-Nahhas, leader of the Wafd Party. Egypt's initial commitment to pan-Arabism intensified, less out of deep-seated conviction than as a political vehicle employed by politicians to enhance their own reputations.[84] By 1939 Egypt was playing a more active role in the diplomacy of the Palestine question and attended the St. James conference in London where it rejected the British white paper of 1939, a document that only Transjordan's King Abdullah accepted. Although Egypt's involvement was still inchoate, it was a striking change from a decade earlier when the palace appeared ready to defer to Britain's lead on this issue.

Throughout the 1940s as the Egyptians became involved more deeply in inter-Arab rivalries, they identified even more closely with the Palestinian issue. The creation of the Arab League headquartered in Cairo provided an additional forum to espouse the Palestinian cause and locked Egypt into tough rhetorical positions. During an address at the American University in Cairo in January 1946, Arab League Secretary General Abd-al-Rahman Azzam referred to a Zionism "which the British at first supported with their bayonets, and the Americans with their money, so that Zionism may build a foreign, imperialistic state in an Arab land."[85] In fact, the Arab League served to formalize Egypt's commitment to the Palestinian cause and reduce its room to maneuver. Even before the United Nations passed the November 1947 resolution adopting the partition of Palestine, Egypt had committed itself to resist the application of this process by force.[86]

With the defeat of the Egyptian army in Palestine and the establishment of the Jewish state, the Palestinian issue became intimately linked to Egypt's domestic and foreign affairs. Egypt had reacted pragmatically to the first Palestine war—entering the war only at the last moment and then largely in response to public pressure, the king's sensitivity to Wafdist pressure, and his own desire to thwart Abdullah's ambitions. Nonetheless, the more deeply Egypt became involved and the clearer the magnitude of the debacle, the more difficult the Palestinian issue was to control. Although the palace could use it in an effort to distract public attention from the social and political problems at home and to counter the designs of Egypt's Arab rivals in the region, it was clear that the politicians were becoming increasingly captive to the very force they sought to exploit. Partly through design and partly through circumstance, the genie of Palestine was now out of the bottle. And no one was quite sure how to put it back in.

That events in Palestine could not be confined to the battlefield became evident soon after the war. The army's defeat in Palestine was attributed to the corruption and venality associated with the palace, large landholders, and other traditional elites. In the minds of many army officers, intellectuals, and activists, the failure in Palestine was the result of a rotten society and corrupt values that needed to be reformed if not totally transformed. Events in Palestine, as Nasser himself would later admit, did not cause the revolution, but they provided an important catalyst to mobilize those army officers responsible for the 1952 coup.

However great its failure in the 1948 campaign, by the early 1950s Egypt was well positioned to play the leading role in the Arab political drama over Palestine that was about to unfold. The Egyptians had fielded the largest army and had sponsored the Government of All-Palestine in Gaza under the nominal leadership of Mufti Haj al-Amin al-Husayni. Moreover, as the preeminent member of the Arab League and the largest Arab state, Egypt was expected to take the lead in confronting Israel. And inter-Arab rivalries left the Egyptians, already vying for influence in the region, little choice but to get out front on the Palestine issue. In 1950 Egypt almost engineered the expulsion of Jordan from the League as a result of Abdullah's policies on Palestine.

Nonetheless, it was the revolution of 1952 and the emergence of Nasser that lifted the Palestine issue to a new level of significance in Egyptian foreign policy and identified Cairo closely with the cause. In the immediate period after the coup, Nasser was preoccupied with consolidating his own power base and could not afford to become preoccupied with the Palestine issue. Yet from the beginning, the Palestine issue was bound up with the revolution. The defeat in Palestine and its perceived relation to the need for social and political change in Egyptian society provided much of the grounding for the Free Officers, who organized the coup. The revolution, however, would pave the way for an Egypt more willing and able to play a dominant role in the Arab arena and would contribute to the ideological appeal Cairo was soon to enjoy. The image of a progressive, egalitarian, and independent regime committed to the destiny of the Arabs — an image that the revolution's propagandists were only too eager to propagate — was very appealing to Arabs who felt themselves victimized by the West, their own regimes, and Israel. In the minds of those looking for heros and myths, Egypt quickly became identified with righteous causes, not the least of which was the Palestine issue.

More important than the revolution itself, however, was Nasser's embrace of the Palestine issue and the charisma and power he was capable of generating on its behalf. As Sadat recalls in his memoirs, "it was Nasser who filled the Arab world, and the world at large, with the name of Palestine." To what extent Nasser was emotionally captivated by the Palestine issue and his own rhetoric is impossible to determine. He devoted a long and eloquent section in his *Philosophy of the Revolution* to the meaning of the Palestine problem, and his addresses are filled, as one would expect, with fiery and emotional references to the "sacred cause." As an Arab and Muslim he undoubtedly felt sincere emotional ties to Palestinian Arabs and shared feelings of impotence and humiliation that flowed from Israel's impressive military and political prowess.

The depths of Nasser's personal commitment to the Palestine question, however, is really beside the point. Whatever his emotional stake in the issue, Nasser used the ideological power of the Palestine cause and the struggle against Israel to present himself as an Arab nationalist par excellence and to push Egypt to the forefront of the political confrontation against Israel, Zionism, and anticolonialism. What better vehicle to counter Syrian and Jordanian influence and try to rid the area of colonialism so Egypt could more effectively exert its own power than commitment to the sacred cause of Palestine? As I pointed out earlier, the Palestinian issue embraced the two major themes Nasser sought to promote — Arabism and anticolonialism. The relationship between Palestine and imperialism was particularly important in Nasser's campaign. Although Arab unity remained an elusive goal and was difficult to define in concrete terms, the problem of colonialism was one that was much easier to understand. Moreover, it allowed the Arab regimes to focus on an external threat and to blame the lack of social and economic progress — if not the failure of Arab unity itself — on a variety of foreign forces — Europeans, Americans, and Zionists. Referring to Palestine, Nasser wrote, "The imperialists intended this territory to be a barrier dividing the Arab East from the Arab West, and a constant drain on the energy of the Arab nation, diverting it from positive construction."[87] After Nasser's nationalization of the Suez Canal and his fortuitous success in withstanding Israeli, British, and French pressure at Suez, Egypt was viewed by many as the Arabs' chief shield against Israel and imperialism and as the prospective liberator of Palestine.

As with Jordan, however, self-interest and ideology mixed uneasily in Nasser's conception of the Palestinian issue. There is little doubt that he exploited and used the cause as ammunition against Israel, the West, and, perhaps most important, at home in an effort to legitimize his own authority. Yet, in large part this calculated and deliberate effort flowed from Nasser's perception of his own role as well as Egypt's place in the Arab scheme of things. Egypt's raison d'être, as Nasser defined it, was, for practical and ideological reasons, linked to its mission as leader of the Arab nation. Thus, Arabism and the Palestinian issue became inseparable — natural allies in Nasser's quest for a special role for Egypt to play. The irony, of course, was that special responsibilities created special burdens that became increasingly heavy for Egypt to bear. Nasser's increasingly militant posturing on the Palestinian issue, despite his efforts to control the PLO and to prevent it from dragging Egypt into an untimely war with Israel, reduced his room to maneuver and challenged him constantly to outbid his Arab rivals on this issue. This kind of posturing helped to create tensions leading to both the 1956 and 1967 conflicts.

Egypt's Palestinian burden became all the more cumbersome and unmanageable following Egypt's humiliating defeat in 1967, the loss of Sinai and Gaza, and the emergence of a more independent PLO leadership that refused to defer to Nasser's timetable or tactics for confronting Israel. The conflict was particularly evident shortly before Nasser's death when in July 1970 he accepted the U.S.-sponsored initiative of Secretary of State William Rogers, which sought to end a war of attrition against Israel that he had initiated. The move was interpreted by Palestinians as implicit Egyptian endorsement of the principle of a negotiated settlement with Israel and raised fears that the most important Arab confrontation state was opting out of the conflict. Whether Palestinian fears were justified and Nasser was indeed moving toward a more pragmatic view of a settlement with Israel will never be known. Within three months he was dead of a heart attack.

That Nasser chose to embrace the Palestinian issue in his quest for influence and power should not obscure the fact that there were other options open to his successors. Anwar Sadat initially appeared no less committed to Palestine than Nasser. In the wake of Nasser's death, Sadat was in no position to take issue with any of Nasser's policies. And in a 1972 article in *Foreign Affairs*, he hammered home the themes that had characterized the Nasser era, particularly Egyptian support for the Palestinian cause.[88] In response to King Hussein's announcement of his United Arab Kingdom plan for the West Bank, Sadat severed relations with Jordan. Without Nasser's pretensions of committing Egypt to a role of regional hegemony, however, Sadat ironically maintained a flexibility and pragmatism that ultimately enabled him to demonstrate Egypt's political and military prowess in a way that had eluded his predecessor.

In October 1973 Sadat initiated a military and political campaign that achieved a level of Arab unity and power that Nasser had never attained. But unlike Nasser, whose conception of Egypt's pan-Arab role locked him into a maximalist strategy without ever possessing the resources to achieve his goals, Sadat pursued a course, at least from 1973 onward, that was geared to more carefully calculated political, economic, and strategic realities. Sadat's strategy was a risky one; yet, he clearly had a more realistic appreciation of his limitations and strengths than his predecessor. He had no illusions of seeking Egyptian hegemony in the Arab world or, for that matter, leading an Armageddon-like struggle against Israel. Indeed, Sadat recognized that to achieve his goals he needed the tactical flexibility denied him by Nasser's commitment to pan-Arabism, anti-imperialism, and Palestinian rights. In short, he required cooperation from conservative states such as Saudi Arabia, political leverage from "imperialists" such as the United States, and, ultimately, a deal with pan-Arabism's archenemy Israel to get what Egypt needed. The 1973 war enabled Egypt to set this strategy into motion. Within four years, Sadat, determined to reap the economic and military benefits that peace with Israel and "full partnership" with the United States would bring, decided to launch his Jerusalem initiative – a move that made him a pariah throughout the Arab world.

Sadat's dramatic trip to Israel in November 1977 was not simply a result of a carefully calculated and cynical political game. It also represented a move that Sadat, at least at the outset, genuinely believed encompassed Egypt's commitment to Palestinian rights. There is no reason to believe that Sadat's commitment to the Palestinian issue was any less genuine than Nasser's. Sadat's changing perception of the Palestinian issue was not a question of a winnowing commitment to the cause but more a reaction to Nasser's definition of that commitment. Indeed, what changed in the decade following Nasser's death was the role the Palestinian issue and its larger pan-

Arab dimension played in Egypt's own scale of priorities. Arabism Nasser-style was never the only competitor for Egypt's ideological soul. It competed with a strong sense of Egyptian identity that was present generations before Nasser was born. And, Sadat, for a host of reasons, including his own inability to compete with the larger than life charisma and appeal of his predecessor, accentuated these trends by minimizing Nasser's pan-Arab commitments and reducing the threat Egypt posed to other Arab states. This new approach allowed Egypt to expand its relations with key Arab states and to pursue a more pragmatic policy toward Israel— both vital components of Sadat's strategy.

The PLO, with its revolutionary rhetoric and attacks on Egypt's signing of the Sinai II agreement in 1975, clearly made Sadat's strategy more palatable at home. Palestinian terrorism against Egypt, most notably the murder of *Al Ahram* Editor Yusuf Siba'i in 1978, allowed the government to highlight a feeling that many Egyptians had sensed for quite some time—that Egypt had already sacrificed too many of its sons and too much of its resources in an elusive quest on behalf of Palestinian revolutionaries that was doing neither Egypt nor the Palestinian people much good. At Siba'i's funeral, the Egyptian prime minister was said to have remarked, "No more Palestine after today."[89]

Although the Palestinian community and the PLO accused Sadat of betraying their cause, it was clear from Sadat's behavior during the period from 1977 to his death that he had not turned his back completely on the Palestinian cause. Sadat had no illusions that his trip to Jerusalem would lead Israel to surrender the West Bank and establish a Palestinian state or homeland. But he was certain that the course the PLO was pursuing and its veto power over any process that fell short of its goals was a sure recipe for disaster. From the beginning, Sadat must have rationalized that he would do as much as he could for the Palestinians but would not allow the agendas of others—the PLO or Israel—to prevent Egypt from accomplishing its territorial goals. He devotes a large portion of his address before the Knesset to the problem, and stated that any peace agreement had to be based on the "achievement of the fundamental rights of the Palestinian people and their right to self-determination, including their right to establish their own state."[90] In the early stages of the negotiations, Israeli Foreign Minister Moshe Dayan recounts in his memoirs, Sadat insisted that he would never accept a separate peace until the Palestinian problem was resolved.[91]

Sadat's critics accuse him of using the Palestinian card as a cover to pursue a separate peace. And it seems clear that soon after the autonomy talks formally commenced that Sadat concluded that the gap separating Israel and Egypt on the Palestinian problem was sizable and might not be bridged. Sadat sustained the talks, hoping for progress but also using them as a way to demonstrate to his Arab critics that Egypt was not simply out to regain Sinai at Palestinian and Arab expense. Although it is likely that Sadat genuinely believed this to be the case, he was also determined to let nothing interfere with the return of Sinai. It was easy for him to rationalize that Egypt had done its share for the Palestinians and that Israeli inflexibility, the PLO's maximalist demands, and Jordan's unwillingness to join the autonomy negotiations had combined to prevent the talks from succeeding.

While there is considerable consistency in Egypt's relationship with the Palestinian issue over the last three decades, there has been significant change. Perhaps the most important development is Egypt's changing perception of the Palestinian issue from an opportunity to a serious liability and risk. Nasser used the Palestinian issue well in his bid for authority at home and influence abroad. And although there were dangers in riding the Palestinian tiger, Nasser believed the benefits clearly outweighed the risks. For Nasser, being on the right side of this issue, meaning the pan-Arab side, even if it meant no solution or even future conflicts, was less risky than opting out of the struggle or allowing other Arab states to take the lead.

This was obviously not the calculation of his successors. Nonetheless, they would pay a price for what was clearly a more pragmatic approach. Sadat's belief that Egypt needed a peace with Israel for purely Egyptian reasons turned the Palestinian issue into a serious liability, particularly after it became clear that the Palestinian dimension of his Jerusalem initiative, later formalized in the Camp David accords, would not be fulfilled. By the summer of 1980 even the illusion that the autonomy talks would succeed had been stripped away. And Israeli actions – such as the July 1980 Knesset measures formally annexing Jerusalem, the June 1981 Israeli strike against the Iraqi nuclear reactor, and the July bombing of PLO headquarters in Beirut – proved highly embarrassing to Sadat. The situation grew even worse for Mubarak. Israel's invasion of Lebanon in June 1982 generated an increasing level of anti-Israeli rhetoric and sentiment and dramatically slowed the normalization process. In September 1982 after the massacres at the Sabra and Shatila refugee camps in Lebanon, Egypt brought its ambassador in Tel Aviv home for consultations. By the end of 1985, he had not yet returned.

Thus, for Sadat and Mubarak, the problem of Palestine had become an issue that threatened to diminish rather than enhance Egyptian prestige as it had under Nasser. And, once the peace treaty was signed, it seriously complicated Egypt's relations with Israel and further undermined its ties within the Arab world. Mubarak, untainted by both the personal rivalries that Sadat had created and the stigma of the Jerusalem visit, has been working to find a middle course between Nasser's activism on the Palestine issue and Sadat's retrenchment. The Egyptians have also been more involved in Palestinian affairs and more ready to criticize the Israelis for lack of progress on the Palestinian issue.

Eager to repair its relations within the Arab world, Egypt has been particularly active in exploiting Jordan's decision to restore full diplomatic ties and in supporting King Hussein's call for an international conference based on Resolution 242. Mubarak has apparently decided that active support for the PLO and the Palestinian cause is an effective way to reestablish Egypt's influence within the region and demonstrate to its Arab allies and adversaries alike that the peace treaty with Israel has not dampened Egypt's enthusiasm for supporting Arab causes. As Mubarak noted in his address to the Egyptian National Assembly during King Hussein's visit in September 1984, "We and the Palestinian people are linked by a common destiny. Our struggle in Egypt for the sake of this destiny is a common struggle. . . . The Palestinian issue is the issue of this generation which has spared no sacrifice."[92] In fact, one of the conditions Egypt has set for the return of its ambassador to Tel Aviv is improving conditions on the West Bank and progress on the Palestinian question.

Nonetheless, Mubarak has left himself considerable room to maneuver on this issue and is not about to undermine the peace treaty with Israel or the economic and military benefits of his relationship with the United States for the benefit of the Palestinians. Egypt will continue to work toward a resolution of the problem in conjunction with other moderate regimes such as Jordan. And the normalization process with Israel may ultimately depend on how much progress is made on the Palestinian problem as well as a resolution of the dispute over Taba, the strip of land at the head of the Gulf of Aqaba. But Egypt is unlikely to accept commitments on the Palestine issue, let alone go back to the confrontation line on behalf of the Palestinians. If other Arab states follow Jordan's lead in restoring ties with Cairo, Egypt will have achieved what few observers, including Nasser, would ever have believed possible – the recovery of Egyptian territory, a formal peace treaty with Israel, and a return to the Arab fold – all before the Palestinian problem was resolved.

# 6

## The Arab States and the PLO: Ambivalent Allies

We have suffered from kings, republics, leftists, rightists, progressives, reactionaries – We have suffered from all.[93]

– Khalid al-Hasan

Nowhere is the gap between the Arabs' collective and ideal commitment to the Palestine issue and the pragmatic interests of individual regimes more clearly revealed than in the Arab states' dealings with the Palestinian national movement and its institutional embodiment, the PLO. And nowhere is the dichotomy between Arab words and deeds more difficult to reconcile. Despite their impassioned rhetoric and moral support, key Arab regimes have engaged in bitter political and military confrontations with the PLO – imprisoning and expelling its leaders, muzzling its fighters, and attempting to influence its political institutions. That Arab regimes, as natural allies, have done as much, if not more, to retard the development of an independent and effective Palestinian movement as Israel, its natural adversary, is difficult for Palestinians to accept. This bitter irony is powerfully encapsulated in the story of the 100 fedayeen who reportedly crossed the Jordan River to surrender to Israeli forces in an effort to escape King Hussein's bedouin army during the 1970 Jordanian-Palestinian civil war.[94]

The conflict between the Arab regimes discussed in this study and the PLO has been a constant theme of Middle Eastern politics for the past four decades. From King Abdullah's use of the Arab Legion to help suppress the Palestinian Arab revolt in 1936, to the creation of the PLO itself as a way to institutionalize Egypt's control over the Palestinian issue, the Arab regimes have tried to co-opt, manipulate, and control Palestinian nationalism for half a century. In this context, it is important to understand that the tension between the Arab states and the Palestinians goes far beyond the disputes over the appropriate tactics for dealing with Israel and the personal rivalries between Palestinian and Arab leaders. The conflict cuts to the core of the raison d'être of the regimes and the resistance movement and raises fundamental questions about their contrasting outlooks, needs, and approaches to the Arab-Israeli conflict. The continuity of these tensions is striking. At times it seems that the conflict between Hussein and Arafat is a modern incarnation of the confrontation between Abdullah and the Mufti.

That the tension between the Arab states and the Palestinians stands out as an all too obvious aspect of their relationship does not make it any easier to explain. There is little doubt that Syria, Jordan, and Egypt, among others, have tried to exploit the Palestinian issue and use the PLO as a weapon against Israel and against each other. None of this, however, accounts for the saliency of the Palestinian cause or the PLO's remarkable ability to bounce back from devastating defeats at the hands of both Israel and the Arab states. Nor can it explain the relatively consistent level of moral, political, and financial support that the Arab regimes have provided to the PLO — support that has allowed the PLO to retain what limited independence it has in the inter-Arab arena and to pursue policies that often conflict with these regimes. The conflicts between the regimes and the Palestinian movement are deep-seated and bitter. Yet it is also clear that these tensions occur in a complex environment that resists one dimensional explanations.

Several factors make the Arab states' relationship with the PLO a difficult problem to analyze. First, the ongoing conflicts between key Arab states and the PLO occur in the context of an Arab world that is generally supportive of and sympathetic to Palestinian national aspirations and committed, within certain limits, to promoting Palestinian goals. The Arab states have the physical power to impose their will on the PLO and bring it to heel. And if the relationship between them was simply a test of strength, the regimes would have been able to crush the PLO years ago. The problem, however, is considerably more complicated. The Arab states have an emotional tie to the Palestinian issue and a commitment to their own constituents, who share an affinity with the Palestinians as fellow Arabs – victimized not only by Israel and the West but by the regimes themselves. Moreover, the nature of Arab politics imposes certain obligations and burdens on each regime, particularly with regard to the Palestinian issue, that are almost impossible to ignore. Although competing for influence in the Arab arena meant playing the Palestinian issue as good politics, the regimes did not create the problem. They were forced to accommodate Palestinian nationalism precisely because it encompassed values that had acquired a powerful hold in Arab political life. Although the regimes manipulate these values, they are also influenced by them in ways that help to promote an even closer affinity with the Palestinian issue.

Second, to confuse matters further, the most dramatic examples of conflict between the PLO and the regimes – Black September, Black June, or the latest Syrian-Fatah confrontation – appear to punctuate relatively long periods of cooperation, however uneasy they may be. During these periods, Palestinian and Arab state interests appear to coincide and even demonstrate considerable compatibility before they are complicated once again by another crisis. Egypt, Syria, Jordan, and the PLO have demonstrated an almost unlimited capacity to set aside bitter differences and cooperate for their mutual interests temporarily. Although this pattern of conflict and accommodation is dictated primarily by the quickly changing alignments within the Arab world and by the sudden crises that create them, it is nonetheless a strange process to observe. The sight of Salah Khalaf, reported head of the PLO terrorist organization Black September that was responsible for killing Jordanian Prime Minister Wasfi Tal, embracing King Hussein at the November 1984 Palestine National Council meeting in Amman was almost surreal.

Third, the PLO's dependence on the Arab regimes and the regimes' need for Palestinian support serves as a balancing mechanism that has prevented permanent breaks and increased the odds in favor of reconciliation even after the most severe confrontations. The PLO deals with the Arab states from a position of weakness. And Palestinians, dependent on the regimes for the bulk of their political, financial, and military support, are forced to accommodate their interests to those of their Arab supporters. For example, Sadat's dramatic decision to seek peace with Israel caught the PLO off guard and forced the Palestinian movement into a closer alignment with Syria. By 1984, however, Syria's efforts to control the PLO and the emerging relationship between Egypt and Jordan compelled Arafat to strengthen his ties with both Cairo and Amman. Although the prospect of an Arafat-Assad rapprochement now seems remote, it cannot be ruled out. Because of the PLO's almost organic dependence on Arab support and the shifting pattern of inter-Arab alignments, the Palestinian movement simply cannot afford permanent ruptures with regimes that can advance or benefit their interests. This desire to offend the fewest possible supporters and burn no bridges has been the hallmark of Arafat's policies for three decades.

To some extent, the same principle is at work in the regimes' relationship with the Palestinians. Although Egypt, Jordan, and Syria can afford to take risks with respect to the PLO and can at times completely ignore Palestinian interests, they cannot afford to disassociate themselves permanently from the Palestinian movement. Whether in the case of Assad for whom support of Palestinian nationalism is a symbol of his defense of Arab nationalism or, more recently, in the case of Mubarak for whom support is a device that can be used to repair relations with the Arab world, the regimes are forced to deal with the PLO. At times the commitment is undertaken voluntarily. It was after all the Arab states who conferred the mantle of Arab legitimacy on the PLO by confirming it as the sole legitimate representative of the Palestinian people a decade ago. And it was King Hussein, who had reluctantly agreed to the Rabat decision, who recently helped to strengthen Arafat's authority by agreeing to host the Palestine National Council in Amman.

It is remarkable in this regard how quickly the Arab states can reverse their roles as allies and adversaries. During Black September of 1970 or Black June of 1976, it would have been difficult to envision that a reconciliation between the PLO, Syria, or Jordan would have been possible. Although these role reversals result primarily from shifting Arab alignments, they also derive from the anomalous position of Arab regimes that are forced to support and suppress the PLO at the same time. On one level, the confrontation between the Arab states and the Palestinians has acquired all the characteristics of unhealthy family relations in which parents mistreat their children only to make amends short of a final break. The children, in turn, dependent on their parents, have little alternative but to absorb the punishment. This "all in the family" mentality produces a bitter ambivalence on the part of both parties.

One thing, however, is clear. The Arab states discussed in this study – their public expressions of support for the PLO notwithstanding – have drawn a distinction between the idea of the Palestinian issue and the reality of an independent Palestinian national movement. Historically these regimes have consistently espoused support for the Palestinian cause and have been generous in supporting the PLO. Yet the Arab states have been determined to ensure that this support does not conflict with their particular interests and that the PLO's objectives remain subordinate to their own goals. This approach has resulted in a wide discrepancy between what the regimes are prepared to say in defense of the Palestinians and what they are prepared to do.

Although it is not always easy to compartmentalize the Arab states' reaction to the Palestinian issue in such a fashion, the gap between rhetoric and action is always present. For key Arab states defending Palestinian rights from the sidelines, bankrolling the PLO and pleading their case in world capitals and international forums had its risks, but was generally low cost. In fact, in relation to the investment, championing the Palestinian issue proved remarkably productive both domestically and in the Arab arena. As Nasser discovered, the power of the Palestinian issue could be a useful vehicle in boosting his personal appeal at home and abroad. Talk is cheap, and in the Arab world, as in other highly charged political environments, it frequently becomes a useful substitute for action. The stream of rhetoric, summit conferences, and communiqués emanating from Arab capitals on behalf of the Palestinians between 1948 and 1967 demonstrates how important this war of words had become to the regimes.[95] It is true that the words were often accompanied by support for PLO operations against Israel, but even here the regimes were determined, particularly after 1967, to prevent the PLO's military operations from dragging them into an unwanted or untimely war with Israel.

The Arab states' reaction to a politically organized, relatively independent, and militant Palestinian movement proved to be much more complex than the more diffuse issue of espousing support for the cause of Palestine. By 1967 the Palestinian problem was no longer as malleable an issue and an Egyptian-backed PLO no longer as passive an actor. A more activist approach had emerged, represented by organizations such as Fatah and the Popular Front for the Liberation of Palestine (PFLP), which had agendas of their own. The diverging tactics became evident in the wake of Israel's stunning military victory in 1967 and the fedayeen efforts to take up their own armed struggle against Israel in the form of cross-border attacks from sanctuaries in Jordan, Lebanon, and Syria. The popularity of the Palestinian call to arms, set against the military failure of the regimes, made it impossible for the latter not to support their cause. These regimes, particularly Jordan's, were now faced with the problem of dealing with the costly economic and political consequences of Israeli military retaliation. Hussein's comment following his army's support of the fedayeen in their battle with the Israelis at Karameh in Jordan in March 1968 that "we are all fedayeen" could not hide the mounting tensions with the Jordanian regime.[96]

Equally important and dangerous, particularly for Jordan and for Lebanon, the PLO began to provide an alternate focus of identity for hundreds of thousands of Palestinian refugees residing throughout the confrontation states and in the Persian Gulf. The fact that the Palestinian leadership was no longer as willing to define their struggle only in terms of broader pan-Arab objectives and began to focus on narrower Palestinian goals was a serious problem for the Hashemites and the Egyptians, who were in no position to take the lead in any campaign to liberate Palestine. Before 1967 one of the secrets of Hussein's success was his ability to convince Palestinians on the West Bank that their interests could best be served by deferring to a Jordanian timetable and tactics.[97] In Lebanon, the presence of hundreds of thousands of refugees and an entrenched PLO would strain the precarious political and confessional balance and push Lebanon into civil war. Even in Egypt, which had a comparatively small Palestinian community, Nasser came to regard the fedayeen and Arafat in particular as a challenge to his authority and prestige in the Arab world.[98]

It was not so much that the fedayeen were so successful. In many respects their military performance and political organization were more amateurish and disorganized than that of their Arab patrons. Nonetheless, they began to fill an important vacuum that had been created in the wake of the abysmal Arab performance in the 1967 war. In contrast to the empty rhetoric of the regimes and their do-nothing summits, the Palestinian militants offered a romantic and uplifting call to action in defense of Palestinian and Arab honor. Although Jordan and Egypt looked for ways to diversify their strategy and adopt more realistic political tactics, the Palestinians, supported heavily by a militant Ba'thi regime in Syria, advocated a popular armed struggle and undying opposition to any nonmilitary solution of the Arab-Israeli conflict. At a time when Arab regimes required tactical flexibility in their dealings with Israel, the Palestinians not only insisted on a rigorous adherence to maximalist goals but on accelerating the Arab timetable for liberating Palestine.

As the differences over tactics intensified and the PLO began to play a greater role in the domestic affairs of the regimes, the feeling of bitterness and betrayal began to intensify. The regimes were naive in believing that the resistance would defer to Arab interests and refrain from intervening in their affairs. And the Palestinians were foolish to assume that Arab slogans of support for Palestinian unity and rights would somehow protect them from regimes that were determined to safeguard their own interests even at the expense of bloody confrontations with the Palestinians. Within 10 years of the 1967 war, every regime on the confrontation line with Israel, with the exception of Egypt, had engaged in violent and sustained confrontation with the Palestinian movement. And in 1977, Egypt, in what was interpreted by Palestinians as the most traumatic blow of all, moved to make peace with Israel.

What made the emerging conflict between the regimes and the Palestinians so bitter and enduring was that it hinged not only on differences in tactics and personalities but on opposing agendas and priorities. The Palestinians were landless, dependent on external sources of support, divided amongst themselves, and willing to take considerable risks to change the status quo. The confrontation states, particularly after the 1973 Arab-Israeli war, were far more interested in strengthening state authority and promoting economic development than in taking risky military initiatives on behalf of the Palestinians. This was particularly true for Egypt and Saudi

Arabia, which were eager to preserve and consolidate the gains they had achieved in the October 1967 war. Even Syria, which had the greatest stake in maintaining its image as a confrontation state and was most hostile to the idea of a separate accord with Israel, moved to accept a disengagement agreement with the Israelis. Two years later Syria moved directly against the PLO in Lebanon out of fear that a Palestinian/leftist alliance there could threaten its own stability and authority.

Thus, the conflict between the regimes and the Palestinians cuts to the core of their respective interests. On one hand, established and conservative regimes, unsure of their own authority and burdened with formidable economic, political, and social problems, confront a highly decentralized movement of national liberation that controls no territory and is committed to changing the status quo in fundamental ways.[99] The gap between the PLO and the regimes on tactics and strategy becomes all the more obvious the closer these regimes are to the confrontation line with Israel. It is one thing for the Libyans and South Yemenis to spout radical rhetoric about liberating Palestine and to support radical Palestinian groups. It is quite another thing for regimes with something to lose to engage in reckless anti-Israeli activity on behalf of the Palestinians. Each state that shares a border with Israel is acutely aware of its own military limitations and wary of allowing an independent Palestinian movement to set into motion political and military developments that the state cannot control. Israel's invasion of Lebanon in 1982 has doubtlessly convinced the Syrians that the PLO can never again be permitted to develop a large and independent military infrastructure in Lebanon.

Although the PLO has been influenced by this establishment mentality and has long ago stripped itself of any truly "revolutionary" character, it is an organization that is committed to what can only be described as a radical and revolutionary change — the establishment of another state in a highly volatile region.[100] None of the states discussed in this monograph are opposed to the fulfillment of Palestinian national aspirations or are theoretically against the creation of a Palestinian state. In fact, all have argued at one time or another that perpetuation of the status quo, with no resolution of the Palestinian problem, presents an even greater threat to their interests. Nonetheless, neither Syria, Jordan, nor Egypt can accept a solution to the Palestinian problem that results in an independent entity operating outside of their sphere of influence. This is particularly true for Syria and Jordan. For these states, the concept of self-determination applied to the Palestinian issue essentially means that the Palestinians have the right to determine their future not in accordance with some abstract notion of inalienable rights but in accordance with these regimes' concrete political and security interests. The Palestinian problem does not exist in a vacuum, and it is naive to expect that a solution will not have to be reconciled with the interests of the Arab states, let alone Israel. No Arab state that shares contiguous borders with Israel can afford to sit back and adopt a laissez-faire attitude on this issue. For varying reasons, Egypt, Jordan, and Syria have all taken a vital interest in the ultimate disposition of the West Bank and Gaza. And they all are determined to ensure that the PLO's pursuit of self-determination and whatever lies at the end of that road are compatible with their own domestic and foreign policy concerns.[101]

Relations between these regimes and the PLO over the past decade and a half have been a series of variations on this basic theme. As the PLO became more independent and insistent on defining its own priorities, the Arab states became even more insistent that the Palestinians respect their interests. The regimes were determined to ensure that the PLO and Palestinians everywhere understood the full consequences of opposing the establishment and the emerging dominant order. In 1970 the Arab states provided little concrete assistance as King Hussein's bedouin army crushed the "Palestinian revolution" in Jordan, and in 1976 the Arab states sat on the sidelines as Syria brought the resistance movement to heel in Lebanon. Within six years the Arab world watched impassively again as the PLO was caught between the Israeli hammer and the Syrian anvil in Lebanon. In both cases Jordan and Syria drew red lines in Palestinian blood to let the PLO know that it had gone too far.

It would be misleading, however, to assume that Arab states have employed force and coercion alone to control the PLO and keep it in line with their own interests. Black September and Black June are only the most dramatic manifestations of a process of carrots and sticks that has been employed to manage and contain the Palestinian issue. Since 1948, Egypt, Syria, and Jordan have searched for a way to institutionalize the Palestinian national movement, to co-opt it, and to make it a more pliable entity deferent to their own interests. Money, political support, military aid in the struggle against Israel, and recognition have all been used toward this end. Jordan has tried to cajole and entice the PLO to join its team by highlighting Jordanian access to the West Bank, the king's prominence in U.S. and Israeli diplomatic strategy, and the promise of a confederal framework. Egypt has sought to use its preponderant influence in the Arab world to tame the PLO's volatile tendencies. And, finally, Syria has sought to convince the PLO that only from a Syrian-led united front can the Arabs hope to achieve their territorial and political goals. Whatever the differences in the approach toward the Palestinian issue, these states are bound by a common objective: to ensure that Palestinian national interests remain compatible, if not subordinate, to their own concerns.


**Jordan and the PLO: The Ultimate Challenge**

Nowhere has this process been more clearly demonstrated than in the relationship between the Hashemite Kingdom of Jordan and the PLO. For the Hashemites and for Jordan's Palestinian majority, the emergence of an independent Palestinian movement with its own political and military agenda presented three challenges that had to be managed and reconciled with Jordanian interests: cross-border attacks into Israel, an alternate and rival source of identity for the East

Bank's Palestinian majority, and an independent claimant to the West Bank. Between 1967 and 1971 King Hussein had considerable success dealing with the first problem and has managed it effectively ever since. The final two challenges, however, cannot be easily overcome and have provided the basis of the conflict between Hussein and Arafat for the past two decades. It is important not to lose sight of these tensions, particularly in view of the Jordanian-PLO dialogue on working out a modus vivendi to recover the West Bank. They raise fundamental questions about whether Jordan and the PLO can ever reach an agreement on a solution to the Palestinian problem acceptable to both parties.

From the outset, Hussein was as hostile to Fatah and as suspicious of the newly created PLO as his grandfather had been of the Mufti and the Arab Higher Committee. Unlike Abdullah, however, Hussein could not afford to run his own Palestinian policy in complete disregard of Arab and Palestinian interests. For Jordan, both the Egyptian-backed PLO and more independent groups such as Fatah and the PFLP not only threatened to drag Jordan into an unwanted military confrontation with Israel through their policy of cross-border raids, but also competed with Hussein for the loyalties of Palestinians on the East and West Banks. Hussein supported the creation of the PLO in 1964. But it was no coincidence that he tried to persuade the Palestinians to hold their first congress on the shores of the Dead Sea rather than in East Jerusalem.

It was clear even before Fatah laid claim to the leadership of the PLO in 1968 that Jordanian and Palestinian interests were almost certain to collide. Hussein had tried to curtail fedayeen activity from Jordan into Israel well before the 1967 war. Fatah never tired of pointing out, particularly during periods of acute tension with the Hashemites, that the first Fatah fighter to fall in action was killed not by Israel but by a Jordanian patrol.[102] Nonetheless, with Jordan's humiliating defeat and loss of the West Bank in 1967, Hussein was in no position to confront the fedayeen. Having ensconced themselves in Jordan following the Israeli capture of the

West Bank, the fedayeen began to step up cross-border operations. Despite the fact that on occasion the Jordanian army provided artillery support for the guerrillas and, in March 1968, fought alongside of the fedayeen at Karameh, it was clear that Hussein could not allow the Palestinians to operate with impunity in Jordan. Not only were the costs of Israeli retaliatory raids rising as civilian casualties mounted and Jordanian economic interests were undermined, but the fedayeen were creating their own state-like infrastructure in the refugee camps that could be used to challenge Hussein's control and authority. Both the PFLP and Democratic Front for the Liberation of Palestine (DFLP) saw great utility in laying the groundwork for a direct challenge to the monarchy.[103] By mid-1970 the Jordanian army had already clashed with the fedayeen on several occasions, setting the stage for the events of September 1970.

Black September constituted a watershed in Jordanian-Palestinian relations. The king's crackdown on the fedayeen ended their autonomous military and political presence in Jordan and established a precedent that every Arab regime has continued to respect: the Palestinian movement would not be permitted to challenge the authority of an established Arab state. Although the conflict was sparked by the PFLP's hijacking of three international jetliners, two of which were flown to the Jordanian desert, Hussein clearly used the incident as an opportunity to move boldly against the Palestinians — something he had probably contemplated doing over the preceeding two years. What is striking about the Black September episode is not that the king finally moved against the Palestinians, but the degree to which other Arab states were unwilling to challenge Hussein's efforts to crush the fedayeen. Although Nasser's diplomatic efforts with Hussein probably prevented the Palestinians from being destroyed completely, most Arab states did little or nothing to support the fedayeen. Iraq, with thousands of forces stationed in Jordan, did not make a move to assist the Palestinians, and even Syria — the only Arab state to provide concrete military support — balked at any major intervention to bail out the fedayeen. For the Palestinians, Black September was a devastating lesson in Arab power politics and a clear example that, whatever their public professions of support, the regimes would not intervene to prevent another Arab state from crushing a Palestinian challenge to its authority. A decade and a half later when the Syrians moved to undermine Arafat's authority and drive him from Lebanon, the Palestinians would again discover the limited nature of Arab support.

Although the king's campaign against the guerrillas in 1970–1971 and the smashing of the PLO's independent infrastructure in Jordan would end the Palestinians' military threat to Jordan, the Palestinians would continue to pose a threat to Hashemite interests. The challenge did not derive from the PLO's military prowess nor from the terrorist campaign it pursued against Jordanian interests in the wake of Black September. The real problem for the Hashemites was much more subtle and linked to the increasing popularity and legitimacy of the PLO both within the Arab world and on the West Bank. Hussein could not afford to allow another force, particularly one that contained elements dedicated to his demise, to provide a focus for Palestinian nationalism on the West Bank, let alone for Palestinians on the East Bank. Yet by 1974 Yasir Arafat was already a rival to the king on both sides of the Jordan River. Hussein's 1972 federation plan for uniting both banks led to Hussein's further isolation within the Arab world and from the Palestinians. Moreover, the Rabat decision of 1974 undermined Hussein's hopes and plans for an active and assertive Jordanian-brokered solution to the Palestinian problem.

Since 1975 the basic theme in Jordanian-PLO relations has revolved around Hussein's efforts to contain and co-opt Palestinian nationalism and to ensure that the PLO does not interfere with his political and security interests. Paradoxically, much of this has been done in the context of an improving relationship with Arafat, particularly after 1979 when the PLO chairman visited Amman for the first time in nine years. Unlike Abdullah, Hussein did not believe he could eliminate Palestinian nationalism by suppressing and subordinating it to a larger Jordanian national identity. The king believed that there was room to accommodate a separate Palestinian identity within a Jordanian framework. Such a framework would enable him to maintain his political and security interests on the West Bank and defuse the force of Palestinian irredentism among East Bank Palestinians.

For Hussein, the mechanism to co-opt and accommodate the challenge of Palestinian nationalism lay in a variation of his grandfather's plan to unite the two banks of the Jordan River. Whether Hussein believes he can reassert full Jordanian control and sovereignty over the West Bank is beside the point. He has convinced himself that Jordan must play a vital role in the ultimate disposition of the occupied territories to guarantee the stability and long-term survival of the Hashemite kingdom and to defuse a Palestinian national movement that is irredentist in nature. Within this general objective, the king has developed a confederal approach based on his March 1972 United Arab Kingdom Federation Plan. In broad terms, the idea of a confederation of two states linked within a joint framework tries to accommodate Palestinian national identity and a desire for national self-expression and independence but reserves for Amman the power to control defense and foreign policy. From the PLO's point of view this would be difficult to accept. Yet, from Hussein's perspective, it may well constitute the only way to guarantee that Jordanian interests can be protected.

## Syria and the PLO: Ally and Adversary

It is perhaps one of the bitterest ironies of Palestinian history that the PLO's most consistent patron and the staunchest defender of militant Palestinian nationalism should also turn out to be its most determined adversary. Not only was Syria one of Fatah's earliest supporters, but also, in contrast to Jordan or Egypt, Damascus sponsored a stream of fedayeen activity in Lebanon, across the Jordanian border, and even from Syria itself. Moreover, unlike Jordan or Egypt, Syria was directly involved in Palestinian politics, creating Sa'iqa in 1968 and actively supporting a number of PLO groups. In material support to the resistance movement, Syria outdistanced almost every other Arab regime. It was no coincidence that Fatah's first military operation – an attack against Israel's national water carrier project – was launched with Syrian backing.

Syria's support, however, came at a very high price. Dependence on Syrian military assistance and Syria's reputation as a confrontation state meant that the Palestinian organizations were also expected to follow Damascus' lead on Arab-Israeli issues. By 1969 Arafat and PFLP leader George Habbash had already seen the inside of Syrian prisons. Tensions between Syria and Fatah, however, were manageable during the 1960s and early 1970s when Fatah's primary emphasis was on armed struggle. In fact, Arafat banked heavily on Syrian support to counter what he believed to be a Jordanian-Egyptian drift toward a negotiated settlement with Israel. Syria was also the only Arab state to assist the fedayeen in their struggle with Hussein in 1970.

Nonetheless, by the early 1970s the Syrian-PLO relationship began to change in important ways. As Assad began to consolidate his own power, the PLO was confronted with a powerful Syrian leader determined to play a major role in the region. Assad's strategy focused less on the unconventional military tactics of supporting national liberation movements pushed by his Ba'thist predecessors and more on the consolidation of Syria's conventional forces. Such an approach envisioned a role for Palestinian fighters, but largely as an appendage of Syrian policy, not as an independent or key component. In fact, Assad was very concerned about the dangers that an independent PLO could pose in the event it pulled Syria into an untimely or unwanted war with Israel. It was Assad, after all, who refused to provide the Palestinians with air support during their conflict with Hussein in the fall of 1970.

There was little doubt that the emergence of a powerful Syrian leader, the PLO's increasing need to assert its independence, and the PLO's drift into Syria's sphere of influence in Lebanon foreshadowed major problems with Damascus. It was not that Assad was any less sympathetic to Palestinian goals than his predecessors had been. Yet he was determined to assert Syrian hegemony in the Lebanese-Palestinian arena—an objective that made it essential for him to bring the PLO to heel. This goal became even more important in the years following the October 1973 war as Egypt and possibly Jordan appeared to be considering separate political arrangements with Israel. Thus, Assad moved to form a coordinated front with Jordan and the PLO. At a time, however, when the Palestinians needed tactical flexibility to deal with the post-October situation, Assad began to demand that the PLO stick even more closely to Syria's agenda.

It was not over the Arab-Israeli peace process, however, that Syria first clashed with the PLO but rather over Lebanon. Although Assad's decision to intervene militarily in Lebanon on the side of the Maronite Christians against the PLO and Lebanese Left must also be seen in the broader context of regional developments, Syria was primarily concerned with Lebanese developments, particularly with a Palestinian movement that refused to defer to Syrian interests. Assad's concern went well beyond matters of prestige. The PLO's presence in Lebanon, its inevitable involvement in Lebanese politics, and particularly its alliance with the Muslim Left threatened to upset the internal balance of power, force Israel into a closer relationship with the Maronites, and perhaps drag Syria into a war with Israel. Moreover, the Palestinian-Lebanese alliance was being supported by Iraq and Egypt, Syria's erstwhile enemies. Should the PLO's support for the Lebanese Left bring a radical Sunni Muslim regime into power in Lebanon, Syria's own domestic stability and the survival of the minority Alawite regime could be threatened.

Once Syria committed its own forces in Lebanon in the summer of 1976, crushing the Palestinian-leftist challenge became a matter of principle. Whatever the political risks of moving against the PLO, Assad could not allow the Palestinians to defy Syria's interests in his own backyard and compromise his prestige in the region. If the Palestinian resistance movement had the audacity to defy Syria in Lebanon and look to others for support, what might it do on broader Arab-Israeli issues? For Assad, it was as if the PLO had betrayed Syria and gone outside of the "family" for support. In July 1976 in a speech justifying Syrian intervention in Lebanon and his confrontation with the Palestinians, he reflected this bitterness:

> How much have we sacrificed for the Resistance in the past few years? Fifty per cent of the Syrian military aircraft destroyed in clashes with the enemy [Israel] before the 1973 war were in the defense of the position of the Palestinian resistance. Thirteen planes were lost in one day in Urqub in defense of the Resistance . . .We lost 500 soldiers in one day . . .Who has done for the Resistance what Syria has done?[104]

This same feeling that an ungrateful PLO had betrayed a self-sacrificing Syria provides much of the basis for the current personal feud between Arafat and Assad. Assad bristled at the PLO's accusations that Syria acted ineptly or half-heartedly in its confrontation with Israel during the 1982 Israeli invasion.

Although Syrian-Palestinian relations improved in the aftermath of the Lebanese civil war and Syria once again began to support the PLO in southern Lebanon, the mutual suspicions and bitterness remained. By 1977 Egypt's decision to withdraw from the confrontation line with Israel and the growing Palestinian dependence on Damascus pulled the PLO deeper into the Syrian orbit and enhanced Assad's leverage, particularly in the political arena. There was clearly an overlapping interest as the PLO needed support to strengthen its position in Lebanon, to counter Egypt's peace with Israel, and to check the possibility that Jordan might be lured into the Camp David process and undercut the PLO's role on the West Bank.

Nonetheless, by 1980 Syrian-PLO interests were again

diverging. Syria's decision to support Iran against Iraq led to Assad's increasing isolation within the Arab world and clashed with Arafat's policy of maintaining broad ties with his other Arab patrons. Moreover, Arafat had a strong interest in maintaining a dialogue with Hussein in an effort to co-opt and perhaps participate in a Jordanian initiative to recover the West Bank. Assad, however, was more determined than ever to ensure that the PLO did not participate in any Arab peace initiatives that did not have Syrian approval. And the Syrians, rather than face almost certain Arab criticism for their support of Iran, boycotted the Arab summit in Amman, in 1982, pressuring the PLO to do the same while mobilizing Syrian forces along the Jordanian border. This was the first Arab summit the PLO had ever missed and reflected how vulnerable Arafat had become to Syrian pressure.

It was again over Lebanon, however, that Syria and the PLO would clash. This time, however, Assad would try to assert his control over the Palestinian national movement in an unprecedented fashion. The PLO-Israeli confrontation in Lebanon, beginning during the July 1981 mini-war in the south and culminating in the Israeli invasion a year later, only exacerbated the differences in tactics and strategy that had come to separate Syria and the PLO. Events in Lebanon also opened a new chapter in the personal animosity between Assad and Arafat. At stake was nothing less than Syria's determination to ensure that on major political and military matters, the PLO defer to Damascus. Arafat's decision to negotiate a cease-fire in Lebanon in July 1981 without Syrian concurrence, his charge during the invasion that Syria had not supported the PLO, and the Arafat-Hussein dialogue in April 1983 over a joint response to President Reagan's initiative all convinced Assad that Arafat was prepared to act directly against Syrian interests and had to be checked. Syria's decision to expel Arafat from Damascus in June 1983 and Assad's support for the Fatah mutiny in the summer set the stage for the confrontation between Fatah and pro-Syrian Palestinian groups that preceded Arafat's second forced exit from Lebanon in December 1983. Moreover, Arafat's decision to meet with Mubarak immediately following his exit from Tripoli further dampened the prospects for reconciliation with Syria and set the stage for the bitter Syrian-PLO tug-of-war that culminated in Arafat's decision to convene the Palestine National Council in Amman in defiance of Syria and some of his own PLO colleagues.

The extent to which Assad has been willing to go to undermine Arafat's authority suggests that meaningful reconciliation between Fatah and Damascus will be difficult to achieve. Despite the intensity of the rivalry, however, most Palestinians within the PLO, including Arafat, believe it is essential to improve relations with Syria and to capitalize again on Syria's political and military power in an effort to further Palestinian goals. The key question, of course, is on what basis any reconciliation can be achieved. The Syrians cannot accept a PLO that has its own agenda and is willing to cooperate in a joint venture with Jordan or Egypt to further its goals at the expense of Syrian interests. Assad's blistering attack against the "two twins" – Arafat and Hussein – before the opening of the eighth Ba'th Party congress in January 1985 reveals how little room remains for reconciliation.[105] And the PLO will be hard pressed to accept Syrian tutelage and blatant interference in its affairs. The only hope for any reconciliation would rest on broadening the focus of diplomatic efforts to resolve the Arab-Israeli conflict to include a comprehensive settlement, including the return of the Golan Heights and a framework for handling the Palestinian issue that gives Syria a major role. Even this, however, is not likely to satisfy Syria's aspirations for leadership in the area or temper its determination to exert a decisive influence in Palestinian affairs. Moreover, there is the personal animosity between Assad and Arafat. Damascus will not accept any resolution of the Palestinian problem that accords Jordan the preeminent role or allows any Palestinian homeland to emerge that does not defer to Syrian interests in the area.

## Egypt and the PLO: Diverging Interests

On the surface it appears that Egypt's ties with the PLO have been far less stormy than the PLO's relations with Syria or Jordan. Cairo never had a violent and sustained military confrontation with the Palestinians along the lines of Black September or Black June, and, consequently, much of the bitterness that characterized the PLO's relationship with Amman and Damascus is absent from Egyptian-Palestinian relations. Even Sadat's decision to make peace with Israel—once regarded as the most treacherous of all acts by an Arab regime—is now rationalized away by the mainstream PLO leadership as Sadat's aberration rather than a change in Egypt's support for the Palestinians. Moreover, the absence of a large Palestinian population, Egypt's own political stability and self-confidence, and its relative detachment from the intimate historical and geographic ties that have bound Syria and Jordan to the Palestinian issue have further minimized the tensions with the Palestinian movement. Nasser's embrace of the Palestinian cause in his own search for regional influence also demanded that Egypt maintain a relatively consistent level of moral and political support for the cause. Palestinians across the political spectrum were generally swayed by his charisma and by their belief that Egypt would play a vital role in supporting their movement and helping them liberate their homeland.

None of this, however, should obscure the tension and problems that have plagued Egyptian-PLO relations for two decades. The basic theme that runs throughout Jordan's and Syria's relationship with the Palestinian national movement also characterizes Egypt's ties. Cairo tried with varying degrees of success to subordinate the PLO's goals to its own definition of what constituted Egyptian and Arab interests. This process was evident from the inception of the Palestinian movement itself. The creation of the PLO in 1964 was largely an Egyptian effort to counter Syria's support for the more militant Palestinian groups such as Fatah and to attempt to institutionalize the Palestinian movement so that it could not drag the Arab states into an unwanted war with Israel. Moreover, unlike Syria under the Ba'th Party, Nasser had little interest in embracing the concept of a popular war of liberation in which the fedayeen would play a leading role. Although during the early 1950s Egypt backed terrorist activity against Israel from Gaza, by the 1960s Nasser had clamped down on Egyptian support for these activities. However intense and militant the rhetoric, Nasser pursued a cautious policy in regard to supporting Palestinian military and terrorist activity in the years before the 1967 war. Unlike Syria or Jordan, Nasser never permitted the Palestinians to use Egypt as a sanctuary for attacks against Israel.

In the period before the 1967 war, however, the tensions between Egypt and the PLO were largely subsumed beneath a general coincidence of interests based on the militancy of Cairo's own position toward Israel and the lack of an independent, popular, and organized Palestinian movement. In the wake of Egypt's humiliating defeat by Israel and the rising popularity of the fedayeen, Egyptian-PLO interests began to diverge in significant ways. For Nasser, the idea of a militant Palestinian movement willing to act independently of his leadership had always been a potentially dangerous and volatile element that could restrict his own room for maneuver. As Egypt sought to examine ways to regain control over territory lost to Israel in the 1967 war, the PLO's nuisance value and potential embarrassment to Nasser increased considerably. Egypt's acceptance of UN Resolution 242 all but formalized a basic divergence in tactics with the PLO and Syria, the latter rejecting all nonmilitary solutions to the Arab-Israeli conflict. Moreover, there is little doubt that Nasser resented the new-found prestige and popularity of the fedayeen and considered the PLO something of a political rival. In any event, Palestinian willingness to act against Israel must have been a painful reminder of Egypt's own inability to score any military or political successes against Israel.

Although during 1969–1970 Nasser supported the fedayeen and the importance of an active "Jordanian front" against

Israel while he waged his own war of attrition, it was clear by mid-1970 that Egyptian-PLO interests were about to collide. Nasser's willingness to consider the Rogers initiative highlighted the dilemma he now confronted with regard to the Palestinians. Although Nasser doubtlessly supported their maximalist goals in principle, Egypt's own interest in regaining Sinai and Gaza pushed him into direct confrontation with PLO objectives.

Nowhere was this ambivalence toward the PLO better demonstrated than in Nasser's reaction to the Black September crisis that broke out shortly before his death. Nasser's efforts to press Hussein to conclude a cease-fire with the Palestinians in late September almost certainly saved them from complete destruction. Yet, it was clear that Nasser had no intention of providing material support for Arafat, let alone actively intervening in the fedayeen's campaign to topple the king. Not only did Egypt have a stake in preserving its alliance with Jordan, but Nasser had no desire to risk a confrontation with Israel or the United States. Although Nasser felt uncomfortable as he watched his ally Hussein smash the fedayeen, he probably took some satisfaction in seeing the PLO's prestige and authority weakened and its military and political power undermined at a time when Nasser himself was considering backing away from his confrontation with Israel. The reversal of roles was striking. As Malcolm Kerr has observed, the supreme irony of Nasser's career was that "he died in the act of shielding his old enemy Husayn, at the expense of his old clients, the Palestinians."[106]

Egypt's conflict with the PLO, however, would reach a peak under Anwar Sadat. It was clear as early as Hussein's second crackdown on the fedayeen in the summer of 1971 that Egypt would not necessarily follow Nasser's efforts to intervene with the king. Sadat participated in a joint mediation effort with the Saudis to work out a compromise that would have allowed the guerrillas to operate in Jordan under limited circumstances, but Egypt was not willing to stake its prestige in pushing a proposal that neither side was likely to accept. As far as Sadat was concerned, the Jordanian-

Palestinian rivalry only drained Arab energies and distracted the confrontation states from the more important struggle against Israel. Although Sadat did not abandon the Palestinians after Nasser's death and continued to support the PLO, he was not about to tie Egypt's interests exclusively to a movement whose goals even Nasser had come to regard as unrealistic. In abandoning Nasser's quest for regional power and influence, Sadat invariably adjusted the role Egypt was expected to play on behalf of the Palestinian cause.

It would take the October war and Sadat's policies toward Israel in the years that followed to demonstrate how dramatically Egyptian-PLO interests could diverge. Paradoxically, PLO leaders had high hopes for Sadat and even greater regard for his decision to take Egypt to war in October 1973. Sadat's decision to support the PLO at Rabat as the sole legitimate representative of the Palestinian people further strengthened the Palestinians' belief that he had no intention of using his military victory against Israel to move ahead separately on the political front at the expense of the PLO.

Yet it was precisely this issue that constituted the basis of the PLO-Egyptian rift in the years following the second Sinai disengagement accord of 1975. Although Sadat appeared to support the Rabat resolution of November 1974, he had some months earlier, during a meeting with Hussein, endorsed the king's right to speak on behalf of the Palestinians on the East Bank – an indication that he was prepared to accept a different interpretation of the volatile issue of who should represent the Palestinians. Although he never actively sought to strip the PLO of this right, it is clear that he did not feel bound to tie Egypt's national interests to the vagaries of PLO politics and the maximalist nature of the resistance movement's ideology. Without movement in the peace process, however, the question of Arab state representation of the Palestinians remained academic.

Sadat's decision to go to Jerusalem triggered Egypt's most bitter conflict with the PLO. Sadat's thinking on the Palestinian issue was much more complicated than his critics would later admit. His primary objective was not to undermine the PLO's legitimacy or to cut a separate deal with Israel. In fact, Sadat probably calculated that at a later stage of the process he could facilitate the PLO's or Hussein's entry into the negotiations. And it was not so much that Sadat embarked on a course to cut the PLO out of the process, he simply moved past it in an effort to achieve a peace with Israel that he considered to be vital to Egypt's political and economic welfare.

As the Arab states and the PLO moved to ostracize Egypt and the gap with Israel on the meaning of Palestinian autonomy became apparent, the importance of finding a legitimate Palestinian representative to participate in the peace process increased dramatically. Neither West Bankers nor King Hussein, however, would risk endorsing even the Egyptian conception of the Camp David autonomy negotiations. The absence of a credible Palestinian partner forced Sadat into the impossible position of appearing to represent the Palestinians himself – a role that only intensified his conflict with the PLO and its Arab supporters. Although Sadat probably never believed Egypt could play this role throughout the negotiations, he was not about to sacrifice Egyptian interests for a PLO that he believed was still incapable and unwilling to see the wisdom of his Jerusalem initiative. Sadat would never formally renounce Egypt's support for the PLO and even maintained contact with the PLO representative in Cairo long after the signing of the peace treaty, yet the Egyptian-PLO political war proved long and bitter. It would take nothing less than Sadat's death, an Egypt committed to reintegration within Arab ranks, and an Israeli and Syrian campaign to crush the PLO in Lebanon to prepare the groundwork for gradual reconciliation with the mainstream Fatah organization. Still, almost nine years after Sadat's initiative, the issue of relations with Egypt remains controversial within the Palestinian movement. And for Mubarak as well, Arafat's PLO continues to be a necessary but troublesome partner in Egypt's efforts to broaden the Middle East peace process and its own ties to the Arab world.

# 7

# Conclusion

My conclusion from all of this is that the Arabs must give up daydreaming and apply themselves to realities.
— King Abdullah

What then are the practical consequences of the Arab states' ambivalence toward the Palestinian issue and particularly toward the PLO? And what does this portend for the future of the Arab-Israeli conflict?

First, now that Egypt is in the process of being accepted back into the Arab and Palestinian fold, it seems clear that it was possible for an Arab state to conclude a formal peace treaty with Israel in advance of substantive progress on the Palestinian issue and still maintain its Arab credentials. It is remarkable that Cairo has been able to reconcile its traditional, idealized commitment to the Palestinian cause with its own pragmatic interests and still maintain these Arab ties. Whether Egyptian-Israeli relations will improve dramatically without future progress on the Palestinian question is another matter. Yet Egypt's balancing act so far is a testament to the prestige and weight Cairo carries in the Arab world and to the willingness of other states to regularize relations with Egypt gradually while it maintains ties with Israel. Although Arab states can rationalize, as the PLO does, that it is important to reintegrate Egypt into Arab ranks in an effort to draw Cairo away from the Camp David accords, these states are also admitting that Sadat's "transgressions" can be forgiven.

Second, while there may be lessons in Egypt's experience with the Palestinian issue, it cannot serve as a model for other Arab states to follow. Egypt had the sense of urgency, the incentive, and the power to move into negotiations with Israel without assurance that the Palestinian problem or the territorial requirements of the Jordanians and Syrians would be met. Moreover, Sadat's strong and charismatic leadership and the successful crossing of the Suez canal in October 1973 provided the necessary context for such a move. Neither Jordan nor Syria possess all of these key ingredients. Hussein sees some urgency in a settlement but lacks the power to go it alone. Moreover, in contrast to Egypt's position on Sinai, Jordan cannot separate the issue of West Bank territory from the political fate of the area's inhabitants. Assad, on the other hand, probably has the power to deal with Israel separately but sees little urgency in a settlement. In fact, it may well be in the interests of his minority-based Alawite regime to hold out rather than to risk a compromise settlement that would undermine Syria's image as the defender of Palestinian and Arab rights.

Third, although the rather sizable gap between Arab rhetoric and action on the Palestinian problem and the regimes' ambivalence toward the PLO should suggest some flexibility on ways to resolve the conflict, it more often leads to a hardening of positions and to inaction. The desire to pursue alternative political arrangements that depart from the formula of direct PLO representation and an independent Palestinian state does exist, particularly in the case of Jordan. When it confronts the strength of the "Arab consensus" on this issue, however, this desire runs into the harsh political and security risks of moving without broad Palestinian and Arab support. What results is a kind of politics of the lowest common denominator in which regimes such as Syria are able to define and enforce a consensus that prevents individuals breaking from the ranks. The PLO, recognizing that it has considerable leverage in these matters, adheres to a hard-line position that leaves little room for individual states to maneuver. Even if there are elements within the PLO that are willing to consider a more flexible approach, as evidenced in Arafat's decision to cooperate with Hussein, it is extremely difficult to develop a consensus within the Palestinian community to support such an initiative.

Fourth, the gap between an Arab state's rhetoric and action on the Palestinian issue virtually guarantees conflict with the PLO. The states discussed in this study are placed in the somewhat anomalous position of supporting the principles of Palestinian self-determination abroad while taking steps to deny Palestinians freedom of maneuver at home or in the region at large. Although the Arab regimes and PLO can accommodate a certain amount of this kind of tension and contradiction in their relationship, they cannot eliminate it. Because of the legitimacy that the regimes derive from supporting the Palestinian cause, they cannot ignore the PLO. Nor can they afford to support the PLO's stated objectives — an independent Palestinian state and the tactical leeway to try and achieve it.

What invariably results are the roller coaster relationships between Arab regimes and the PLO. These relationships, characterized by broad swings between cooperation and confrontation, have been extremely difficult to normalize. For states like Syria and Egypt, which are powerful enough to play their own roles in the Arab-Israeli conflict, the ambiguities in their relationship with the Palestinians are easier to reconcile. For Jordan, however, whose identity as a nation and approach to a negotiated solution of the Arab-Israeli conflict is inextricably linked to the Palestinian factor, tensions with the PLO are not as easy to manage. Traditional mistrust and suspicion and legitimate debates over current policy have prevented the kind of agreement between Hussein and the PLO that is probably necessary to pave the way for negotiations with Israel. The problem is highlighted in the February 1985 framework agreement between Jordan and the PLO. The language of the accord is sufficiently vague to allow both Arafat and Hussein to attach their own interpretations on the key issues of who will represent the Palestinians in negotiations and what they will be negotiating for. Nonetheless, the PLO, suspicious of the king's motives and wary of the gap between Jordanian principles and practices on the Palestinian issue, cannot be flexible enough to allow Hussein to move into negotiations on terms Israel would accept. Whether Jordan, which has come closer than any other Arab state in working out a modus vivendi with the PLO on a negotiating framework, will be able to bridge this gap remains to be seen.

Fifth, the nature of the relationship between the PLO and its Arab supporters ensures that any resolution to the Palestinian problem will have to occur on several levels. Even before an Arab state, most likely Jordan, could deal successfully with Israel on this issue, it would have to resolve tensions in its relations with other Arab regimes, particularly Syria and the Palestinian community. Jordan cannot move into negotiations with Israel without Arab backing and PLO support. And the need to gain the support or at least acquiescence of these two groups severely restricts its room to maneuver with Israel. In fact, at a time when maximum flexibility is required to deal with Israel, any potential Arab interlocutor would be heavily engaged in assuaging these other two constituencies – a fact that is certain to produce an ambiguous or harder-line negotiating position. Nowhere is this clearer than in Jordan's current efforts to bring Syria into the peace process – an objective that has introduced a range of complicating factors, including an international conference, the Soviet Union, and Syria's own ambiguous position on negotiations and territorial compromise.

The irony of the moderate Arab predicament on the Palestinian issue is clear. Egypt and Jordan have an all too realistic assessment of their limited capacity to further Palestinian goals, but have become prisoners of their own rhetoric and idealized professions of support for the Palestinian cause and the PLO. Having publicly articulated these positions for almost 40 years at home and abroad, and having so closely linked the Palestinian cause to their own political credibility and prestige, it is now extraordinarily difficult to compromise, let alone to abandon the cause. The religious overtones of the problem embodied in the Jerusalem issue and the psychological and political importance of redeeming Arab honor have made it even more difficult for the Arab states to extricate themselves from the problem. In fact, the advantages of trying to close the gap between an idealized and practical solution to the Palestinian problem, as sought by King Hussein, may not outweigh the risks of being accused of betraying Palestinian goals.

Thus, moderate Arab regimes – those that attach some degree of urgency to a resolution of the Palestinian problem and a negotiated settlement of the Arab-Israeli conflict – are trapped in a tightly bound circle that is difficult to break. Egypt, Jordan, Saudi Arabia, and the smaller Gulf states perceive the dangers of an unresolved Palestinian issue. Yet they are trapped between the rhetoric of the past and the necessity of surviving in a volatile Arab arena in which they are exposed and vulnerable. Thus Syria, which sees little urgency in negotiations, exploits this vulnerability to ensure that it controls the pace and focus of any peace process.

In an effort to resolve their dilemma and to reconcile this idealized view of the Palestinian issue with their own interests, moderate Arab states have looked to Israel and the United States for the concessions that would make this process less painful and threatening, as well as for support against hostile and radical forces. In the end, however, most of the initiative to bridge the difference between what is and what is not possible on the Palestinian issue will probably have to come from the Arab states and Palestinians themselves. Much progress has already been made. Yet it is by no means certain that any Arab state will risk redefining the Arab consensus on an issue that is inextricably linked to that state's own political credibility at home and its prestige in the Arab world. And, perhaps from both necessity and circumstance, these states may remain burdened by a problem that they can neither ignore nor resolve.

# Notes

1. "Voice of Palestine," June 28, 1928, *Foreign Broadcast Information Service* (FBIS), *Middle East and Africa* (MEA), June 29, 1982.

2. Abu Iyad, *My Home, My Land: A Narrative of the Palestinian Struggle* (New York, N.Y.: Times Books, 1981), xiii.

3. Interview with Salah Khalaf, *Al-Watan al-Arabi*, November 18, 1983, pp. 46–49.

4. Michael Hudson, *Arab Politics: The Search for Legitimacy* (New Haven, Conn.: Yale University Press, 1977), 2–3.

5. Walid Khalidi, "Thinking the Unthinkable: A Sovereign Palestinian State," *Foreign Affairs* 56 (July 1978): 695–713.

6. Gamal Abdel Nasser, *The Philosophy of the Revolution* (Buffalo, N.Y.: Economic Books, 1959), 71.

7. James Jankowski, "Egyptian Responses to the Palestine Problem in the Interwar Period," *International Journal of Middle Eastern Studies* 12 (1980): 24.

8. Aaron S. Klieman, "The Arab States and Palestine," in Elie Kedourie and Sylvia G. Haim, *Zionism and Arabism in Palestine and Israel* (London: Frank Cass, 1982), 118–136.

9. Barry Rubin, *The Arab States and the Palestine Conflict* (Syracuse, N.Y.: Syracuse University Press, 1981), 172.

10. Fayez A. Sayegh, *Arab Unity: Hope and Fulfilment* (New York, N.Y.: The Devin-Adair Co., 1958), 160–161.

11. Fouad Ajami, "The End of Pan Arabism," *Foreign Affairs* 57 (Winter 1978/1979): 308.

12. Yehoshafat Harkabi, *Arab Attitudes Toward Israel* (Jerusalem, Israel: Keter Publishing, 1972), 382.

13. Speech by Houari Boumediene, April 29, 1978, *Journal of Palestine Studies* 28, vol. 7, no. 4 (Summer 1978): 195-196.

14. Interview with King Hussein, Amman Television Service, January 2, 1984, FBIS/MEA, January 4, 1984.

15. Malcolm Kerr, *The Arab Cold War: Gamal 'Abd al-Nasir and His Rivals, 1958-1970* (London: Oxford University Press, 1971), 134-135.

16. Albert Hourani, *Syria and Lebanon: A Political Essay* (London: Oxford University Press, 1946), 100.

17. Quoted in Harkabi, *Arab Attitudes*, 70.

18. M. T. Mehdi, *Peace in Palestine* (New York, N.Y.: New World Press, 1976), 15.

19. Interview with Assad, Damascus Television Service, December 24, 1983, FBIS/MEA, December 27, 1983.

20. Khalidi, "Thinking the Unthinkable," 697.

21. Interview with King Hussein, Amman Television Service, March 17, 1984, FBIS/MEA, March 8, 1984.

22. Uriel Dann, *Studies in the History of Transjordan, 1920-1949: The Making of a State* (Boulder, Colo.: Westview Press, 1982), 1-4.

23. Joseph Nevo, "Abdallah and the Arabs of Palestine," *The Wiener Library Bulletin* 31, nos. 45-46 (1978): 51.

24. Dann, *Studies in the History of Transjordan*, 11.

25. Kenneth W. Stein, *The Land Question in Palestine, 1917-1939* (Chapel Hill, N.C.: The University of North Carolina Press, 1984), 192-199.

26. Ann Mosely Lesch, *Arab Politics in Palestine 1917-1939: Frustration of a Nationalist Movement* (Ithaca, N.Y.: Cornell University Press, 1979), 111, 132.

27. Klieman, "The Arab States and Palestine," 125-126. 125-126.

28. Shaul Mishal, *West Bank East Bank: The Palestinians in Jordan, 1949-1967* (New Haven, Conn.: Yale University Press, 1978), 1-2, 5-9.

29. King Abdallah, *My Memoirs Completed: "Al Takmilah"* (London: Longman, 1951), 13.

30. Jon and David Kimche, *Both Sides of the Hill* (London: Secker and Warburg, 1960), 59.

31. Abdallah, *My Memoirs Completed*, 30.

32. Ibid., 30–31.

33. Dann, *Studies in the History of Transjordan*, 11.

34. Aqil Hyder Hasan Abidi, *Jordan: A Political Study 1948–1957* (New York, N.Y.: Asia Publishing House, 1965), 20.

35. Naim Sofer, "The Political Status of Jerusalem in the Hashemite Kingdom of Jordan, 1948-1967," in Kedourie and Haim, *Zionism and Arabism in Palestine and Israel*, 225-273.

36. T. E. Lawrence, *Seven Pillars of Wisdom* (New York, N.Y.: Doubleday & Company, Inc., 1926), 41.

37. King Hussein, *Uneasy Lies the Head* (New York, N.Y.: Bernard Geis Associates, 1962), 13.

38. Mishal, *West Bank East Bank*, 114.

39. *Middle East Record 1967*, 3 (Jerusalem, Israel: Israel Universities Press, 1971), 392.

40. Abdallah, *My Memoirs Completed*, vi.

41. King Hussein address, Amman Domestic Service, November 22, 1984, FBIS/MEA, November 26, 1984.

42. Peter Snow, *Hussein: A Biography* (London: Barrie & Jenkins, 1972), 194-195.

43. Uriel Dann, "The Jordanian Entity in Changing Circumstances, 1967–1973," in Itamar Rabinovich and Haim Shaked, *From June to October: The Middle East Between 1967 and 1973* (New Brunswick, N.J.: Transaction Press, 1978), 233.

44. Susan Hattis Rolef, *The Political Geography of Palestine: A History and Definition* (New York, N.Y.: American Academic Association for the Peace in the Middle East, 1983), 23.

45. King Hussein speech before the Palestine National Council, FBIS/MEA, November 26, 1984.

46. Aaron S. Klieman, *Israel, Jordan, Palestine: The Search for a Durable Peace* (Beverly Hills, Calif.: Sage Publications, *The Washington Papers*, 1981), 25.

47. Interview with Hafiz al-Assad, *Newsweek* (January 16, 1978).

48. Hudson, *Arab Politics*, 257. See also Patrick Seale, *The Struggle for Syria: A Study of Post-War Arab Politics 1945-1958* (London: Oxford University Press, 1965), 1-2.

49. Stephen H. Longrigg, *Syria and Lebanon Under the French Mandate* (London: Oxford University Press, 1958), 23.

50. Zeine N. Zeine, *The Emergence of Arab Nationalism* (New York, N.Y.: Caravan Books, 1973), 59.

51. Ibid., 114.

52. Zeine N. Zeine, *The Struggle for Arab Independence* (New York, N.Y.: Caravan Books, 1977), 25.

53. Ernest Dawn, "The Rise of Arabism in Syria," *Middle East Journal* 16 (Spring 1972):153.

54. Hudson, *Arab Politics*, 256. See also Raymond A. Hinnebush, "Revisionist Dreams and Realist Strategies: The Foreign Policy of Syria," in Bahyat Korany and Ali E. Hillal Dessouki, *The Foreign Policies of Arab States* (Boulder, Colo.: Westview Press, 1984), 283.

55. Zeine, *The Struggle for Arab Independence*, 142.

56. Y. Porath, *The Emergence of the Palestinian-Arab National Movement 1918–1929* (London: Frank Cass, 1974), 71–122.

57. Longrigg, *Syria and Lebanon Under French Mandate*, 113.

58. A. L. Tibawi, *A Modern History of Syria Including Lebanon and Palestine* (New York, N.Y.: Macmillan, 1969), 358.

59. Leila S. Kadi, *Arab Summit Conferences and the Palestinian Problem (1936–1950), (1964–1966)* (Beirut: PLO Research Center, 1966), chapter 3.

60. Seale, *The Struggle for Syria*, 33.

61. John F. Devlin, *The Ba'th Party: A History From Its Origins to 1966* (Stanford, Calif.: Hoover Institution Press, 1976), 52–53.

62. Kamel S. Abu Jaber, *The Arab Ba'th Socialist Party: History, Ideology, and Organization* (Syracuse, N.Y.: Syracuse University Press, 1966), 29.

63. Nabil M. Kaylani, "The Rise of the Syrian Ba'th, 1940–1958: Political Success, Party Failure," *International Journal of Middle Eastern Studies* 3 (1972): 3–23.

64. Devlin, *The Ba'th Party: A History From Its Origins to 1966*, p. 224–225.

65. William B. Quandt, Fuad Jabber, Ann Mosely Lesch, *The Politics of Palestinian Nationalism* (Berkeley, Calif.: University of California Press, 1973), 183.

66. Tareq Y. Ismael, *The Arab Left* (Syracuse, N.Y.: Syracuse University Press, 1976), 37.

67. Yaacov Bar-Siman Tov, *Linkage Politics in the Middle East: Syria Between Domestic and External Conflict 1961–1970* (Boulder, Colo.: Westview Press, 1983), 129–130.

68. Ismael, *The Arab Left*, 37.

69. Hafiz al-Assad speech, March 8, 1974, *Journal of Pales-*

*tine Studies* 3, no. 4 (Summer 1974).

70. Aryeh Y. Yodfat and Yuval Arnon-Ohanna, *PLO Strategy and Tactics* (New York, N.Y.: St. Martin's Press, 1981), 38.

71. Ahmad Khuli, "Arafat and Us," Part II, *Tishrin*, Damascus, July 9, 1983, FBIS/MEA, July 15, 1983.

72. Ibid.

73. Hafiz al-Assad speech, Damascus Syrian Arab News Agency (SANA), January 3, 1985, FBIS/MEA, January 4, 1985.

74. Anwar el-Sadat, *In Search of Identity* (New York, N.Y.: Harper & Row, Publishers Inc., 1977), 200.

75. Israel Gershoni, *The Emergence of Pan-Arabism in Egypt* (Tel Aviv, Israel: Shiloah Center for Middle Eastern and African Studies, 1981), 84–88.

76. Jankowski, "Egyptian Responses to the Palestine Problem in the Interwar Period," 1–38. See also William L. Cleveland, *The Making of a Arab Nationalist: Ottomanism and Arabism in the Life and Thought of Sati'al-Husri* (Princeton, N.J.: Princeton University Press, 1971), 151; Ammon Cohen, "The Beginnings of Egypt's Involvement in the Palestinian Question: Some European Perspectives," in *Asian and African Studies* 16 (1982): 137–145.

77. Quoted in Jankowski, "Egyptian Responses to the Palestine Problem in the Interwar Period," 6.

78. Gershoni, *The Emergence of Pan-Arabism in Egypt*, 37. See also Sylvia G. Haim, *Arab Nationalism: An Anthology* (Berkeley, Calif.: University of California Press, 1962), 49–50.

79. Seale, *The Struggle for Syria*, 19.

80. Albert Hourani, *Arabic Thought in the Liberal Age 1798–1939* (London: Oxford University Press, 1970), 316. See also Haim, *Arab Nationalism*, 49.

81. Jankowski, "Egyptian Responses to the Palestine Problem in the Interwar Period," 20.

82. Ibid., 15.

83. Ibid., 23.

84. Seale, *The Struggle for Syria*, 20–21.

85. Haim, *Arab Nationalism*, 165.

86. Nadav Safran, *Egypt in Search of Political Community* (Cambridge, Mass.: Harvard University Press, 1961), 204.

87. Ismael, *The Arab Left*, 87.

88. Anwar Sadat, "Where Egypt Stands," *Foreign Affairs* 51, no. 1 (October 1972): 114–123.

89. Walid W. Kazziha, *Palestine in the Arab Dilemma* (London: Croom Helm, 1979), 101.

90. *New York Times*, November 21, 1977.

91. Moshe Dayan, *Breakthrough: A Personal Account of the Egyptian-Israel Peace Negotiations* (New York, N.Y.: Alfred A. Knopf, 1981), 161.

92. Husni Mubarak speech, Cairo Domestic Service, December 2, 1984, FBIS/MEA, December 3, 1984.

93. Quoted in Helena Cobban, *The Palestinian Liberation Organization: People, Power and Politics* (London: Cambridge University Press, 1984), 197.

94. Bard E. O'Neill, *Armed Struggle in Palestine: A Political-Military Analysis* (Boulder, Colo.: Westview Press, 1978), 166.

95. Leila S. Kadi, *Arab Summit Conferences and the Palestine Problem*, 187-193.

96. Abu Iyad, *My Home, My Land: A Narrative of the Palestinian Struggle*, 61. See also *New York Times*, March 26, 1968.

97. Mishal, *West Bank East Bank*, 114.

98. Fouad Ajami, *The Arab Predicament: Arab Political Thought and Practice Since 1967* (Cambridge: Cambridge University Press, 1981), 91-92. See also O'Neill, *Armed Struggle in Palestine*, 181.

99. See Kazziha, *Palestine in the Arab Dilemma*, 34-38; Alan R. Taylor, *The Arab Balance of Power* (Syracuse, N.Y.: Syracuse University Press, 1982), 56-61.

100. Fouad Ajami, "The End of Pan-Arabism," 371. See also Gabriel Ben-Dor, *State and Conflict in the Middle East: Emergence of the Post Colonial State* (New York, N.Y.: Praeger Publishers, 1983), 198-200.

101. Gabriel Ben-Dor, "Nationalism Without Sovereignty and Nationalism with Multiple Sovereignties: The Palestinians and Inter-Arab Relations," in Gabriel Ben-Dor, ed., *The Palestinians and the Middle East Conflict* (Ramat Gan, Israel: Turtledove Publishing, 1979), 157.

102. Quandt, *The Politics of Palestinian Nationalism*, 164.

103. Kerr, *The Arab Cold War*, 143-144. See also Ismael, *The Arab Left*, 62-78.

104. Quoted in Adeed I. Dawisha, *Syria and the Lebanese Crisis* (New York, N.Y.: St. Martin's Press, 1980), 171-172. See also Walid Khalidi, *Conflict and Violence in Lebanon* (Cambridge, Mass.: Center for International Affairs, Harvard University, 1979), 82-84.

105. See Hafiz al-Assad speech, Damascus Domestic Service, January 5, 1985, FBIS/MEA, January 7, 1985.

106. Kerr, *The Arab Cold War*, 153.

107. Abdallah, *My Memoirs Completed*, 27.